GETTING ORGANIZED AT WORK

by Dawn B. Sova, Ph.D.

with Robert Gregor

LearningExpress • New York

Copyright © 1998 Learning Express, LLC.

All rights reserved under International and Pan-American Copyright Conventions. Published in the United States by LearningExpress, LLC, New York.

Library of Congress Cataloging-in-Publication Data

Sova, Dawn B.
    Getting organized at work / Dawn B. Sova.
       p. m.—(Basics made easy)
    Includes index.
    ISBN 1–57685–144–3
    1. Office management. 2. Time management. 3. Office layout. 4. Office practice—Automation. I. Title. II. Series.
HF5547.S647   1998
650.1—dc21   98–27450
                                                                                                         CIP

Printed in the United States of America
9 8 7 6 5 4 3 2 1
First Edition

For Further Information
For information on LearningExpress, other LearningExpress products, or bulk sales, please call or write to us at:
    LearningExpress®
    900 Broadway
    Suite 604
    New York, NY 10003
    212-995-2566

LearningExpress is an affiliated company of Random House, Inc.

ISBN 1–57685–144–3

CONTENTS

Introduction．．．．．．．．．．．．．．．．．．．．．．．．．．．．．．．．．．．．v

Section I	Setting Priorities．．．．．．．．．．．．．．．．．．．．．．．．．．．．．．1
Chapter 1	Targeting Your Needs．．．．．．．．．．．．．．．．．．．．．．．．．．3
Chapter 2	Becoming Organized By Design．．．．．．．．．．．．．．．．11

Section II	Organizing Your Time．．．．．．．．．．．．．．．．．．．．．．．．19
Chapter 3	Becoming A Time Tamer．．．．．．．．．．．．．．．．．．．．．．21
Chapter 4	Exploiting Peripheral Time．．．．．．．．．．．．．．．．．．．．33
Chapter 5	Turning The Telephone Into A Tool．．．．．．．．．．．．．41
Chapter 6	Focusing On Professional, Not Social, Tasks．．．．．．．51
Chapter 7	Managing Tasks Effectively．．．．．．．．．．．．．．．．．．．．59

Section III	Organizing Your Desk Environment 69
Chapter 8	Arranging Your Desk Location 71
Chapter 9	Organizing Your Desk 79
Chapter 10	Organizing Your Files 87
Chapter 11	Using Color Coding To Get Organized. 95
Chapter 12	Creating A Place For Everything 101
Section IV	Getting Organized With Technology. 109
Chapter 13	Exploiting the Potential of Fax and E-mail . . . 111
Chapter 14	Organizing Your Computer Files 119
Chapter 15	Eliminating Clutter With Your Computer 129
Chapter 16	Using Spreadsheets To Get Organized 137
Chapter 17	Using The Internet To Get Organized 147
Section V	Merging And Purging Information 157
Chapter 18	Retaining And Removing Records 159
Chapter 19	Destroying Files Safely 167
Section VI	Staying Organized. 173
Chapter 20	Maintenance Tips For Staying Organized at Work. 175
Appendix	Additional Resources 181

INTRODUCTION

What's the problem?

The office manager asks for notes on a report or for the file that you should have returned a week ago. You promise to come up with it—as soon as you plow through the mountain of papers and folders on your desk and the surrounding floor.

"I know where everything is—just give me a little time to find it. Is that so bad? Hey, my desk may be a mess, but I know where everything is."

Does that sound like you? If so, maybe you should slowly replay in your mind the last time that you had to find an important piece of information in your cluttered work space.

Are you impressed with what you remember? Did you look like a polished professional while shoving piles of paper aside, moving boxes, and flipping through folders? Probably not.

Would you prefer to have avoided the stress and frantic searching? If so, then maybe it's time to get organized.

SECTION | 1

SETTING PRIORITIES

No one can organize your work space as effectively as you can. Even professional organizers (who now number more than 1000, according to the National Association of Professional Organizers) can't. They can create a structure, and because they charge for their help, most people try to work within that structure for a time. Sooner or later, however, the old, bad habits return, and out go most of the rules of organization.

If this is true, is there any hope for you? Definitely. You have the advantage of knowing your *specific* organizational needs, and that allows you to develop a system that works for *you*. Determine your organizational needs first, then organize yourself.

CHAPTER 1

TARGETING YOUR NEEDS

A place for everything, and everything in its place.

Sound boring to you? It is. Not everyone can live with a rigidly structured system—and not everyone should. You have to organize your workplace so that it meets your needs in a way that makes you most efficient. If neat little cubbyholes and alphabetically arranged and labeled supplies are what you want, that's fine. Most of us, however, need to personalize the way we organize our personal and professional lives so that they make sense to us.

In this lesson, you will identify your specific organizational needs by assessing the particular problems you face at work. The key to creating an effective plan is to know your strengths and weaknesses—then decide where you need to focus your attention.

WHERE DO YOU BEGIN?

How disorganized are you? Most of us really don't know how disorganized we are, because we can usually put the blame for our stress and frustrations on any number of other workplace problems. While these may contribute to our feelings of being pressured or overwhelmed, they are rarely the sole problem and they often disappear once we take control.

Are you organized enough to complete a routine office assignment? Before you answer, consider how your current state of organization at work would allow you to handle the following hypothetical situation:

Situation 1

You work for a small company, where your duties often overlap with those of the other three people in the office. Some projects require that all four people work with the same set of files, while other projects are handled solo. You have just completed making calls to gather statistics and cost data to organize the first phase of a new project that the company will bid on. Knowing that you had a lot of calls to make and that some of the information would be useless, you wrote everything down on a lined pad. Now, you're ready to enter your findings on the appropriate forms in the project file folders before giving them to the person responsible for completing the next phase of the research for which your information is needed. What do you do?

   a. Get up from your desk, locate the appropriate folders in the alphabetically arranged file cabinet drawer, enter the information, and return the folders to their correct order in the file cabinet.
   b. Pull open the drawers of your desk, grab every file folder on the desk top and see if it contains the project materials, and sort through stacks of files and other materials that surround your desk.
   c. Ask your coworkers if they have the file and look through every folder stacked on their desks.
   d. Give up trying to locate the folders that contain the original documents, run copies of the forms, label a new file folder, and let someone else worry about finding the original folders.

Answer **a** is the ideal situation and one that you can make a reality by creating a plan to deal with your specific organizational needs. Knowing exactly where the files are and that they are immediately available to you removes the stress and confusion of searching for them. You project an image of professional competence and confidence when you simply withdraw the files as needed and enter the information that you worked so hard to gather.

Answer **b** actions will leave you looking and feeling frazzled, and your professional image will suffer. As you search frantically for the information on the one project, you will create an even greater chaos on your desktop as you stack and restack papers, files, binders, and other materials. Even worse, others in the office will see your confusion and question your competence, which can translate into decreased opportunities for advancement.

Answer **c** is also not desirable because your task is the first phase in the project, so you are the first person to enter gathered information into the files. The others are waiting for your data before they can move on to the later phases, so they don't need the files until you have entered your information. Only if you are certain that you did not remove the files and only if you are certain that the files are not somewhere in your work space should you ask someone else about them. Even then, however, resist the temptation to search through someone else's desk and papers.

Answer **d** is tempting but decidedly dishonest and dangerous. The original files probably contain the results of a preliminary investigation of the project that was compiled by one of the company decision makers *before* assigning phases of the research to the office staff. Although copies of the information are probably filed in several other places, you have the responsibility to locate the folder with which you were working.

- Are you satisfied with the way your current work situation would have allowed you to handle the above situation?
- Do you feel effective and capable of handling most ordinary daily situations at work?
- If you were in charge of rating your performance at work, would you give yourself high marks as an employee?
- Do you rate your job satisfaction as high?

A "no" answer to two or more of the above questions means that you are probably not getting the most from your job, and a lack of organization is probably the reason.

WHAT ARE YOUR PROBLEMS?

An out-of-control work life can wear you out mentally and physically and make you feel dissatisfied with your job performance and with yourself. It can also hurt you professionally because, no matter how qualified and capable you are, other people will only see the deadlines that you miss and the information that you misplace.

That might not seem fair, because you do contribute in many valuable ways to the company and provide skills that are unique, yet that is the reality of daily business life. Fortunately, you can improve your professional performance and your professional image as well—if you face your problems openly. Let's start *now*.

Not sure that a lack of organization has hurt you? You'll be surprised with what you learn about the effect of organization on your work performance—if you answer the following questions honestly.

Rating Your Work Efficiency

Identify the number of times each of the following has occurred at work in the past month and place that number on the line after the item.

1. You forgot about or failed to meet a deadline. _____
2. You put off returning a telephone call until "later," then forgot until the person called a second time. _____
3. You forgot about or failed to show up for an appointment or meeting. _____
4. You completed work then misplaced it and had to do the work a second time. _____
5. You misplaced a telephone number or address. _____
6. You spent so much time socializing in the office that you were unable to complete your work. _____
7. You couldn't begin a work assignment immediately because you were missing materials or supplies. _____
8. Your office e-mail account contained duplicate messages from people because you failed to respond to their earlier messages. _____
9. You submitted work that was hastily done and given only your cursory attention. _____
10. You took work home to finish that should have been completed during the regular business day. _____

Total Score _____

Look at the number of times that you have omitted doing an important task at work in the past month and take note of individual categories in which this occurred. You may have only missed one meeting, one telephone call, and one deadline, but each "miss" hurts your image as a professional. You have to show coworkers and business associates that you care about what you do. Even contacts outside of your office are important because the impressions that you create through telephone, e-mail, and personal contact stay in people's memories. These contacts function as networking and, when you are ready to advance in your career, they may result in job offers.

Work that must be completed a second time, files that are misplaced, and telephone numbers that are lost represent time that could be used in a more productive way. If you often feel overworked and overburdened, then your lack of organization may be the problem. Completing a task once the right way is a lot less stressful and time-consuming than having to retrace your steps and to correct errors that could have been avoided.

So what is your score? Let's be blunt about your situation. Any score other than zero shows that you have been unnecessarily inefficient and that some improvement in organization is needed.

If your score is three or less, you probably have fairly good control over your work life, even though you certainly can identify areas of improvement. You know that missing even one deadline—the wrong deadline—can ruin your professional image and make you seem unreliable to others. Forgetting to return even one telephone call or one e-mail message can hurt business relationships and make you an outsider with the wrong people. Missing one appointment or meeting can have devastating professional consequences.

If your score is between four and eight, your level of disorganization is most likely taking personal and professional tolls on you. Being unable to meet deadlines, complete projects, connect with others on schedule, or finish work during the business day may leave you feeling stressed out and overburdened. You probably end each day feeling mentally and physically exhausted. Beyond the personal toll, you may find that your career has remained on hold, rather than advancing at the speed that you had expected. A lack of appropriate organization may be to blame, as well.

If your score is eight or above, your situation is critical and you should decide now to take the steps that can turn around your professional life. You may have a lot of work ahead, but together we *can* improve the situation considerably.

WHAT ARE YOUR PRIORITIES?

This is the time to be brutally honest with yourself. As you review your answers to "Rating Your Work Efficiency," do you think that you have valid reasons for missing deadlines and appointments or for failing to complete work? Not excuses but *reasons* to explain logically that you were in some way prevented by factors outside your control from meeting that requirement?

Many reasons might exist that are valid—although not always acceptable in the workplace. Sort them out, so that you have a clear view of what is really going on—and going wrong—in your life. You might find that these reasons require that you reorganize your personal life in some way, at the same time that you work to create stronger organizational skills in your professional life.

What do I mean by this? And, why mention personal reasons at all? If you are going to set realistic goals and establish priorities, you have to identify all personal reasons that have made you less efficient in the past month or months, to focus attention on the areas that really need work. Why waste time working on problems that won't recur or that have now been resolved?

Many personal situations are temporary, and their negative effects on your work behavior will usually disappear once your personal situation has calmed. We sometimes have a bad month or two in which meetings are clustered within a short time during which family or personal illness or obligations make work difficult. Other personal situations may also intrude temporarily on our professional lives. That's why you have to identify and understand the factors that have gotten in your way.

In reviewing your responses to the efficiency scale, do you find that personal obligations played a role in lessening your efficiency in any *one* category? If this is the case—and if you have not usually had difficulties in that category in the past—then the problem should be resolved when your personal difficulties disappear.

Do not completely ignore this problem, but do focus the major part of your attention on your organizational needs in the areas for which you cannot identify valid personal reasons for poor performance. You are the major player in this enterprise, so take control—the chapters that follow will help you in every area of your professional life.

NEXT STEP

You have gotten off to a great start by identifying the ways in which your lack of organization has interfered with your efficiency at work. In the next chapter, you will separate your strengths from your weaknesses and establish a plan to turn your weaknesses into on-the-job strengths.

CHAPTER 2

BECOMING ORGANIZED BY DESIGN

Getting organized at work requires that you create a system to suit your particular needs. Some of us have difficulty completing work on time, while others run into problems with appointments and meetings. The same organizational solutions can't be randomly applied to everyone because all of us have different needs, which change as our situations change.

Success lies in directly addressing your weaknesses and building on your strengths as you create a system of organization that is right for you right now. You may only need to read those chapters that address your current difficulties, then refer later to others as your situation changes—and that's fine. To be successful, however, you will have to read the entire section dealing with the problem before mapping out a strategy and devising your solutions. In short, you will have to become *organized by design*.

WHAT ARE YOUR GOALS?

What results do you hope to achieve by getting organized at work? Your answers to the "Rating Your Work Efficiency" scale in Chapter 1 should offer a fairly accurate view of the problems that you are experiencing—and the desired results of your design to solve those problems.

To plan effectively, you must first formulate specific goal statements based on what you believe is necessary for you to succeed. To create an effective system, your goals *must* be structured and specific. Statements such as "I hope to become better organized" or "I want to become successful" are too vague for your design. Instead, goal statements must focus directly on your problems at work. Consider the goals on the following page, and place a check next to all those statements that match your desired goals. You will probably add goals to the list, as you think more deeply about your specific situation and recognize additional areas that can be changed.

Now that you have clearly identified your goals, you might think that the only work left is to turn to the appropriate sections and begin to create your design. You will do so soon enough. Before you do, however, you should also identify the effects that others have on you.

Your responses to the work efficiency scale may have left you shaking your head in dismay over the missed meetings and appointments and forgotten telephone calls and e-mail messages. You have probably blamed yourself entirely for all of these problems. Yet, you do care about your job and you know that you have the talent and skill to succeed. So, what's the problem?

Well, you may be disorganized, and that problem may be responsible for less-than-stellar performance at work, but the fault may not be yours alone. Such factors as other people and the general environment of your workplace can present serious obstacles as you attempt to meet your goals. Before you can create a plan that will help you tackle the behaviors that are hurting your progress at work and keeping you feeling stressed out, overburdened, and overwhelmed, you must identify these factors. Why waste time blaming yourself when the fault lies elsewhere? Even more crucial—why waste time focusing solely on changing *your* actions if the problems are external, as well?

WHAT IS YOUR DESIGN?

How much more than simple conviction will it take for you to become organized at work? Let's first identify the areas in which you seem to be weakest. Don't just put aside your responses to the "Rating Your Work Efficiency" scale—study them.

Goals For Gain

_____ I will begin to plan project stages as soon as I receive assignments.

_____ I will return each day's telephone calls before ending my workday.

_____ I will respond to e-mail messages as I read them and, even if I don't have needed information, inform correspondents that I will send a follow-up message.

_____ I will record the date and time of appointments and meetings in a central planner.

_____ I will record telephone numbers and addresses in a central location.

_____ I will inform individuals and organizations immediately if I cannot attend a meeting or appointment.

_____ I will create separate storage areas for works in progress and completed work.

_____ I will maintain an updated inventory of vital materials and supplies.

_____ I will create a production schedule for each project and include time for critical self-evaluation.

_____ I will determine the time that I need to complete individual tasks and adhere to the allotted times.

My Specific Goals:

_____
_____
_____
_____
_____
_____
_____
_____
_____
_____
_____
_____
_____
_____
_____

Which incidents have occurred the most in the past month?

- Are you more likely to miss meetings or appointments?
- Do you habitually forget to return telephone calls?
- Is work often completed late?

As you review your answers, do you see a pattern emerging? Now identify the three areas in which you seem to have experienced the greatest difficulty in the past month:

1. _____
2. _____
3. _____

These are your weaknesses, and you are going to focus attention on developing strategies to turn these weaknesses into strengths.

Now, identify the three areas in which you seem to have been most efficient in the past month:

1. _____
2. _____
3. _____

You have identified the strengths that you already have and that you will use to create your plan to become organized at work.

At this point, you have looked carefully at your work habits and effectiveness, but what about the influence of your workplace environment and the people with whom you work? How do they help or hurt you? Are your coworkers and the environment supportive? Or do you feel as if each workday is a constant struggle?

Take the following brief quiz and locate the often unrecognized problems that others create for many people when they try to get organized at work. Facing these obstacles is vital to creating a successful design.

Creating Your Design Quiz

Answer the following questions about yourself at work to determine which areas need to be a part of your design and which need the most work. Use the following scale to respond:

Strongly agree = 5
Agree = 4
Does not apply or uncertain = 3
Disagree = 2
Strongly disagree = 1

1. My coworkers often interrupt me needlessly while I work. _____
2. My superiors rarely provide me with clear instructions or define goals for the projects that I must complete. _____
3. I frequently spend too much time on the telephone to track down information for others. _____
4. I have no input in determining how my workday or work load is scheduled. _____
5. I am often required to complete work-related tasks during my lunch hour. _____
6. I am frequently left with no time to eat lunch because of work-related tasks. _____
7. I have several times had to delay beginning a project because the needed materials were not available in the office. _____
8. I have several times had to delay beginning a project because I could not locate the needed material that I had gathered previously. _____
9. I have often missed appointments because I misplaced the necessary information regarding time and place. _____
10. I cannot usually find desk supplies when I need them. _____
11. I cannot usually obtain desk supplies from the office manager when I need them. _____
12. I do not have enough desk surface to contain all of the office equipment, supplies, and other materials that I use on a regular basis. _____
13. I post materials and notes on walls in the area surrounding my desk. _____
14. I am not permitted to send and receive fax messages unless first cleared to do so by a superior. _____
15. I do not think that e-mail is a very useful means of communication. _____
16. I have not modified my computer storage files in any way from their default settings. _____
17. I only use the computer for tasks that are directly related to each project. _____
18. I always print out paper copies of all information that I store on the computer hard drive. _____

19. My computer files contain information on projects that go back five years or more. _____
20. I face most office tasks with a great deal of anxiety. _____
21. I do not have the time to devote to becoming organized. _____
22. Nothing that I do now will make any difference in my success at work. _____
23. To be effective, I need every item that is presently in my work area. _____
24. I often do not have the energy to complete all of the work assigned to me on a daily basis. _____
25. My desk is in a high-traffic area with numerous distractions. _____

Are you surprised by your answers? Do you feel somewhat better about your level of efficiency after identifying some of the obstacles that you face?

Your greatest obstacles are contained in those statements to which you responded with a 5 ("Strongly agree") or 4 ("Agree"). They identify your biggest problems and those that have the greatest potential for preventing you from achieving your goals.

To be honest, you will probably not be able to eliminate all 25 obstacles—unless you have total control over your work life. Most of us do not. Instead, we must make the best of a situation that is often made more difficult by incompetent superiors, an uncaring work environment, and the need to keep our jobs.

Even if you can't change everything around you, knowing what stands in the way of your success is still valuable. Even more valuable is for you to know which external factors you can change and which you must simply accept. Why waste time and effort trying to bring about change in areas in which you are powerless? Rather, concentrate your time and energy on what can be accomplished.

However great, your efforts may not have much effect on a superior who provides little direction for the work you are assigned (item 2), the scheduling of your work load (item 4), the availability of materials to complete projects (items 7 and 11), the availability of quick communication (item 14), or where your desk is positioned (item 25).

You can, however, do quite a bit to decrease your anxiety (item 20), to effect change (item 22), and to increase your energy level (item 24). As you address these items and others in the survey over which you *do* have control, you will create a design that will help you to achieve your goal for getting organized at work.

Let's begin.

NEXT STEP

You have identified your on-the-job strengths and weaknesses. In the next section, you will identify the ways in which you manage time and learn how to control your use and abuse of time.

SECTION II

ORGANIZING YOUR TIME

Most of us could benefit from having more minutes in an hour and more hours in a day to do everything that we have to do and want to do. How often do you promise yourself to finish a task or put the finishing touches on a project "tomorrow"? Then "tomorrow" arrives and new work faces you or another uncompleted task grabs your attention, leaving earlier work incomplete and the "finishing touches" undone. Does this sound familiar?

If you don't seem to get as much done as you expected and often wonder where the time in your workday has gone, you need to identify where your minutes go and then resolve to take control of time.

The chapters in this section will guide you in identifying your priorities and show you how to make effective use of your time.

CHAPTER 3

BECOMING A TIME TAMER

Have you ever noticed how much time is spent needlessly searching for misplaced materials, for keys to open file cabinets and desk drawers, for papers that *should* be in a particular place but are not, for telephone numbers, and other data?

Those lost minutes might not seem like much when viewed alone, but add them up and you will see just what you lose each workday, as well as over a week, a month, and a year. The time you waste might fall into categories like the following:

listening to a coworker complain when you first arrive	5 min.
searching for a file	5 min.
visiting the rest room	10 min.
looking at a coworker's pictures while returning from the rest room	3 min.
talking on the telephone with a friend to plan lunch out	5 min.
daydreaming three or four times in a day	15 min.

These few activities represent only some of the ways that time is stolen from the workday—and they waste 43 minutes of time in a day. If you spend your time in relatively the same way each day of a workweek, you will waste 215 minutes—or more than 3 1/2 hours per week. Over a 50-week work year, you will have wasted more than 175 hours—the equivalent of about 22 (eight-hour) workdays!

How do you waste time? How much more could you accomplish in a workday if you organized your time better and turned *wasted* time into *work* time?

Knowledge is power—and this is especially true in regard to time. Before setting priorities, you have to know exactly how you spend the hours and minutes in your workday.

- Has the telephone been devouring your time?
- Do coworkers gnaw away at your available minutes?
- Have insignificant tasks been given too much attention, leaving you to give less attention to the work that truly counts?

In short, *how efficiently do you spend your time?*

WHERE DOES THE TIME GO?

You probably think that you are too busy to analyze where your time goes. Yet, you need to get organized at work, and managing your time is important if you are going to succeed. A big part of managing time is setting priorities. How can you set your priorities if you do not fully know what they are? The truth is that you can't.

An old saying states, "You have to spend money to make money," and the same is true of time. You can afford to devote several hours to gaining control of your time and your life. Once you do, you will be happier and more productive because you will become organized at work, as well.

In which activities do you spend most of your time while at work? Are you *really* completing work most of the time and taking advantage of the hours available to you? Or does much of the day pass with only spurts of work being completed? What do you do during the time that you are not working? Where does your time go?

One way you can answer these questions is to keep track of your time by creating a time journal in which you record everything that you do in the course of each workday over a two-week period. This time frame is necessary to allow you to record and analyze both daily and weekly activities. Periodic tasks, those that must be completed weekly or monthly, should be noted in separate areas of the journal.

In some jobs, each day is relatively the same and consists of typing letters, filing correspondence and reports, photocopying information, making telephone calls, or completing similar tasks. If your job fits this pattern, you can simplify your journal greatly by setting up a chart with columns that are headed by the usual tasks in a day, an example of which appears later in this chapter.

WHAT DO YOU DO?

Although the nature of your job, as well as its responsibilities and duties, will vary according to the company you work for and your job title, the following should provide a guide in setting up your own journal assessment pages.

Let's assume that you work in that same four-person office that appeared in Situation 1 in Chapter 1. You obviously will be distracted by your coworkers' problems and conversations, and your productivity will be affected by those distractions. On visits to and from the rest room you will also be tempted to stop and talk, or you may feel that you are being rude if you refuse to pause in your work and respond to others.

Situation 2

Terry is one of four office assistants in a small company in which the duties of all four people are clearly defined, although their areas of responsibility may often overlap. The office is open and not partitioned, with all four desks and workstations clearly visible to everyone. Each person has a telephone, a computer with a printer, and various file trays on the desk. The four share use of the copy machine, fax machine, and supply cabinet.

On a typical day, all four workers will be required to perform such duties as filing copies of outgoing and incoming paperwork, typing reports and letters, making telephone calls to gather information or respond to clients, and photocopying materials, although the content of these materials may vary. The company allots the employees two daily, 15-minute breaks, one in the morning and one in the afternoon, as well as 30 minutes for lunch. Because the company adheres strictly to start and end times, employees must arrive by 8:30 a.m. and they may leave at 5 p.m., as long as all of the assigned daily work is completed. All typing of daily memoranda and letters as well as all filing must be completed before the employees leave for the day.

On the day recorded in the "Task Assessment Survey," Terry was required to remain until 5:48 p.m. to complete typing client contact letters that should have been ready to send out by midafternoon when the mail delivery arrived. Because this work was not accomplished, the employer required that Terry stay to complete the work, so that it would not carry over into the next workday and create a further backlog.

Could Terry have avoided this disruption in schedule by using time during the day more efficiently? Let's review the survey on page 25 and examine how Terry's work time was managed.

What do you notice first about Terry's day? Here and there, a few minutes are left unaccounted for. That may not be a problem in itself because one task may end and some time is required to settle in before the beginning of the next task. What *does* pose a problem is the existence of substantial unaccounted-for time, such as the 12 minutes between 8:48 and 9:00 a.m., after Terry has ordered supplies by telephone, and the 13 minutes from 10:17 through 10:30, after Terry has finished responding to client calls and before the scheduled break.

Such gaps in time lead to several questions. What was going on during that time? Daydreaming? Talking (undocumented) to coworkers? Doodling?

How can Terry account for a lunch period that should end at 1 p.m., yet the task assessment sheet shows that the work of answering clients' calls does not resume until 1:08? Is this the result of a late return from lunch, or was the employee simply shuffling papers around on the desk to find needed telephone numbers? Whatever the reason may be, these minutes represent wasted time that threw off the schedule of the day, and the result is that all assigned work was not completed by 5 p.m., the usual end of the workday.

Instead of having to spend 48 minutes after quitting time to complete the typing of client letters, Terry could have saved significant time in the day by avoiding several time-wasting activities.

Is the total of 33 minutes in rest room visits a daily occurrence? Was the 13-minute conversation with a coworker important enough to have to stay late at work? What about that eight-minute personal telephone call and the unaccounted-for gaps in time that total 25 minutes?

Even if we ignore the two or three minutes between tasks, Terry clearly wasted 79 minutes—one hour and 19 minutes—that would have been more than adequate time to complete the letters and allow the workday to end on time.

TASK ASSESSMENT SURVEY

Telephone Calls	Paperwork	Photocopying Materials	Typing Reports, etc.	Non-Work	Time Spent (Min)
Ordering supplies					8:30–8:48
					9:00–10:00
		Long report			
				Rest room break	10:01–10:10
Clients					10:11–10:17
				Break	10:30–10:45
	Incoming correspondence				
				10:46–11:45	
	Opening mail			Talking with co-worker	11:46–11:59
				Lunch	12:00–12:29
					12:30–1:00
Clients					1:08–1:12
			Daily correspondence		1:17–2:18
				Personal telephone call	2:20–2:28
	Copies of outgoing mail			Break	2:30–2:45
					2:48–3:30
Clients				Rest room visit	3:31–3:55
		Memos to distribute			3:57–4:10
			Boss's memo		4:14–4:25
					4:28–4:50
			Client letters		4:51–5:48

Did Terry deliberately set out to have to remain almost an hour after the workday should have ended? Of course not—and neither do many of us who find that we have run out of time when we still have work to complete. The real problem is that several seemingly minor interruptions in Terry's work schedule add up to a major loss of time and productivity.

WHAT ARE YOUR PRIORITIES?

The one-day assessment may not reflect a typical day for Terry or for anyone else, but it does provide a fairly good idea of what many of your days *may* contain. Of course, you may really be more productive on some days than on others, as we all are, and the gaps in time that appear in the sample assessment may be nonexistent on those days. Still, if you record your activities in this assessment over a period of two weeks, you will come close to determining how you spend your typical workday.

If your daily tasks vary and if you have specific weekly and monthly responsibilities, you should take a different approach to examining your workday. Rather than arranging the day according to tasks, view your day according to one-hour increments and identify the activities completed within each increment. Assume that you are Kerry, an administrative assistant in a small manufacturing company, and responsible for multiple tasks. Your work hours are supposed to be 9 a.m. to 5:30 p.m., but you are required to stay until all new work for the day has been completed. View the following sample "Time Assessment Survey" as an example.

TIME ASSESSMENT SURVEY

Time	Activity and Minutes Spent	
9:00–9:59	Check voice mail and record messages	(15 min.)
	Check and sort fax messages	(5 min.)
	Distribute fax and voice mail messages	(10 min.)
	Open, sort, and distribute mail	(30 min.)
10:00–10:59	Type invoices and letters	(45 min.)
	Take break	(15 min.)
11:00–11:59	Inventory supplies	(20 min.)
	Make personal call to see if a store has the product you need	(5 min.)
	Talk with coworker about other places to obtain the product	(10 min.)

	Type invoices and letters	(25 min.)
12:00–12:59	Sort and stack incoming letters and reports to file	(15 min.)
	Take a rest room break	(10 min.)
	File incoming reports and letters	(20 min.)
	Locate specified files for manager	(15 min.)
1:00–1:59	Lunch	(30 min.)
	Straighten out desk and locate numbers to return customer calls	(20 min.)
	Type up customer list with product name	(10 min.)
2:00–2:59	Make customer calls	(20 min.)
	File copies of outgoing letters	(10 min.)
	Talk to coworkers for ideas about good area restaurants to entertain guests	(15 min.)
	Check company Web site e-mail for order	(15 min.)
3:00–3:59	Take break	(15 min.)
	Type up Web site orders	(25 min.)
	Meet with human resources manager	(20 min.)
4:00–4:59	Place a telephone order for supplies	(20 min.)
	Take a rest room break	(10 min.)
	Discuss your evening plans with coworkers	(10 min.)
	Type the day's call-in orders	(20 min.)
5:00–5:55	Complete remaining filing	(15 min.)
	Check with supervisors that all work has been completed satisfactorily	(5 min.)
	Retype incorrectly completed call-in and Web site order sheets	(35 min.)

Could those 25 minutes spent after the official close of the workday have been prevented? A quick look at the "Time Assessment Survey" might make you think not, but the reason for this late end to the day is not unexpected work. Instead, work that was not correctly completed earlier in the day had to be redone.

Look at the schedule of the day and locate when the order sheets were first completed. What else was Kerry doing in the same time frame that the orders were also supposed to be completed?

The Web site orders were originally typed in the 3:00–3:59 time frame, after Kerry took a break but before the meeting with the human resources manager. The call-in orders were originally typed up in the 4:00–4:59 time period, after a discussion with coworkers about the evening ahead.

Could these factors have had a negative effect on the quality and accuracy of the work? Was attention to the upcoming meeting responsible for inaccuracies in the transfer of data? Did Kerry rush to gather materials for her meeting or to become mentally prepared to meet with the manager?

How did the rest room break and socializing with coworkers influence the attention that Kerry gave to typing up the day's call-in orders? Was so much thought—and time—given to social concerns that the routine work received only cursory attention?

Anyone who reviews the workday activities recorded in the "Time Assessment Survey" might come to a similar conclusion. The reasons for the belated completion of work might, of course, be entirely different. Many of the orders may have been confusing or Kerry may not have been familiar with new forms being used by the company. Another possibility is that this may be the first time that certain products are being offered, and different procedures might be needed. Many more possibilities also exist.

What would your reaction be regarding your workday if you were Kerry? Would you be pleased with what you see? What roles do a lack of sufficient organization and incorrect management of time play in creating your problems? You will more accurately pinpoint the cause if you follow the advice given earlier in this chapter and assess your work and non-work activities for approximately two workweeks.

Look at how much time you actually spend in non-work-related activities during the workday. What are you doing in that time? Do you really need the 30-minute lunch, two 15-minute breaks, and two 10-minute rest room breaks? Wouldn't you rather leave work on time and relax at home?

If you were Kerry, what could you have done during the time that you spent talking with coworkers about area restaurants and about your evening ahead? If you had put those 25 minutes toward preparing and reviewing the orders, would you have made fewer mistakes?

Review *why* you spent 20 minutes straightening out your desk to locate the telephone numbers that you needed to make customer calls. Why is the information scattered around the desktop? Shouldn't those numbers be kept in a central file so that they are easily accessible?

HOW CAN YOU TAME TIME?

To get organized at work, you have to use time efficiently and, yes, you have to become a time tamer. You cannot allow your work to expand and to fill the time allotted—instead, you have to create a daily itinerary that identifies what you intend to do for every hour of the workday. The unexpected *will* arise and you *will* have to modify your schedule at times, but the basic structure should be maintained.

Use your two weeks of time and task assessment to create that itinerary. The itinerary is important because when supervisors or coworkers come to you with unanticipated demands, you can more accurately explain why you can or cannot accomplish what is needed in the time that is allotted. That will not always eliminate late work evenings, but it may be useful to others who can work with you to devise a reasonable and mutually beneficial solution to the time-crunch dilemma.

If you are going to succeed in getting organized at work, you will have to take several important steps on your own—before you attempt to deal with negative external influences. You—not other people—stand to benefit from becoming better organized, so begin with yourself. Following are several general ways you can tame time and become better organized.

1. **Identify your periods of peak performance.** According to the assessments, when do you appear to be most efficient? Are you a morning person whose energy level is highest at the beginning of the day? Do meetings, appointments, and telephone calls made early in the day seem to be the most successful? If so, try to manipulate your schedule so that tasks requiring more energy and concentration take place in the morning.

    Many people return from lunch and become sleepy within a few minutes of sitting at their desks. Are you one of these people? If so, arrange to complete the most important—and, when possible, the most boring—work before lunch. Save for after lunch those activities that will force you to move away from your desk and walk around. In this way, you can use activity to keep you awake when your body clock runs down.

2. **Schedule your tasks on daily, weekly, and monthly bases.** Identify how you will complete your usual daily tasks. Draw up a schedule in which you name the task and the time of the day (based on your periods of peak performance) that each task should be completed. Also establish a time frame in minutes (or hours, as needed) within which the task should be completed. Be realistic in scheduling so that you can use the results as a guide to the success or failure of your daily (and weekly or monthly) performance.

    Include in your itinerary the amount of time for breaks and for lunch that your employer allows. Be honest and include, as well, the inevitable moments that you spend in socializing, but don't overdo it. We'll discuss in Chapter 6 the role of socializing and how to avoid wasting time in this way. Some socializing can be beneficial to your mental health because it helps to alleviate the pressures in a workday, so include some socializing in the schedule. Too much, however, can have a negative effect on your efficiency at work.

An itinerary is only a guide, and one that is only useful when it contains current information. As your responsibilities change, make changes in your daily, weekly, or monthly itinerary and post them in full sight of your desk.

3. **Remain flexible in completing tasks.** You might combine several tasks or share tasks with others in the office, and this can save you time and aggravation. As you use new equipment or become more adept at completing repeated tasks, the time devoted to these tasks should lessen. If you find that you are spending the same amount of time completing tasks that you have been performing for weeks and even months at a stretch, you might be making the work fill the time allotted to it. Determine if you can combine or even eliminate steps.

On a periodic basis, review the itinerary and revise it by shortening your time frame for tasks that have become second nature to you. If you can accomplish something in 30 minutes rather than the 45 minutes that it once took you, plan to put the remaining 15 minutes to better use. Your increased efficiency will allow you to take on more challenging projects and can lead to greater job security and more chances for advancement.

4. **Get started now.** Stop procrastinating at every point in your itinerary. Stalling for time only leaves you out of time when the workday ends. Use your schedule of tasks as a list of deadlines and decide that they will be met, so that you can end the workday on time.

If your itinerary indicates that you are supposed to open the mail at 9:15 a.m., don't decide to make calls first or to catch up with a coworker's social life. Open the mail at 9:15 a.m.—and stay within the time frame that you allotted to the task.

Of course, the key is to remain flexible and to make up a schedule that works for you and helps you become more organized at work. You may find that you consistently avoid opening the mail as your first task of the day and that you would rather do something else to begin. If your supervisor has given you freedom to decide the order in which you complete work, rewrite the itinerary to reflect your preferences. Different tasks motivate different people. You need to find the one task that will serve as a catalyst to start your day.

5. **Gather and use appropriately marked bins to lessen time lost in confusing paper shuffling.** If your itinerary includes the use of specific files, forms, or other papers on a regular basis, obtain wire boxes to hold each type of paper. At the least, identify an "in" box and an "out" box, to separate the work that will be sent out from the work that must be responded to and filed. You will save considerable time by only having to separate papers once, instead of the several times that will become necessary as you shuffle through and repeatedly mix up the papers. Within each box, organize the papers in order of their importance or in the order in which you must deal with them, then follow through on that organization.

6. **Use technology to keep you on schedule.** Use a personal digital assistant (PDA) to aid you in tracking appointments, providing reminders, managing your calendar, and generally keeping you on top of your schedule. We will review this technology in Section IV, but it bears mentioning here as well.

These devices differ widely in cost, a significant factor to consider. They range from the low-technology electronic organizers that cost around $100 to full-blown PDAs, which include fax, e-mail, and paging features and cost around $800. Your needs and career goals will determine just how organized you can afford to be. The advantage to this technology is that one handheld device allows you to combine many other paper approaches to getting organized at work.

What is *your* best approach to taming time? Only you can answer that question. Your job and responsibilities are key factors to keep in mind as you create a system to manage your time and to become better organized at work. Later in this section, you will identify in detail just what your job involves and analyze how your tasks might be completed with greater efficiency.

NEXT STEP

You have examined the various ways in which you use and abuse time during the workday. In the next chapter, you will learn how to make effective use of time that is usually wasted as you wait during appointments and telephone calls, and while performing other tasks.

CHAPTER | 4

EXPLOITING PERIPHERAL TIME

Peripheral time is time that is wasted while we attempt to complete other important tasks at work. The fault may not be our own, but the time lost lessens our efficiency and forces us to reorganize our schedules if we are going to complete other tasks on time. In short, the ramifications are greater to us than to those who waste our time.

The actual blocks of peripheral time might seem brief, because they typically range from only five minutes to less than a half hour. Taken in total, however, such time may make up a large part of your day and may throw off your organized planning, thus leading to lessened efficiency and lower output. Instead of feeling exploited by tasks that draw time from your day, make peripheral time work for you.

WHERE IS YOUR TIME WASTED?

Are you unsure of the amount of peripheral time that exists in your workday? Think of any time in a day when you are forced to wait idly for a telephone response, to begin a meeting, for an appointment to appear, or for equipment to complete printing or running off copies. This time is peripheral time. How can you handle the time that is spent waiting to complete telephone calls and other tasks when you cannot control that time?

Let's consider several areas in which you might find yourself waiting nervously and thinking of all the tasks that you *could* be completing, while you remain idle and passive and wait for others to respond or for equipment to complete operations. How have you—or would you—react while dealing with the following time-wasting incidents?

Time-Wasting Incident 1

You call a supplier of office products to place an order as part of your usual weekly schedule. The telephone operator for the office products company answers with the company name and, after you state that you want to place an order, demands, "Please hold for a sales representative." You are placed on hold and, 5 or 10 minutes later, you are still on hold. Although you are tempted to hang up and to call the company later, you need to place the order today. What do you do?

   a. Hang up and try back every 15 minutes until you are put through directly to a sales representative.
   b. Shout the following into the receiver as soon as the operator answers: "Put me through immediately to a sales representative. This is an emergency!"
   c. Try the call only once, then call the next company on a list that you have created in advance, moving down the list until one deals with you immediately.
   d. Plan to complete a minor task and wait patiently until the sales representative comes to the telephone, then identify how long you have waited and politely express your displeasure that you had to wait so long.

Time-Wasting Incident 2

You must make many photocopies of a long report, a task that will probably take a half hour or more, even on the high-speed photocopier that also collates and staples. The machine sometimes jams or runs out of staples or paper, so you should stay close by as the copies are run. What do you do?

   a. Take a chance that the machine will perform without difficulties and return to your desk to complete other work.

    b. Ask a coworker whose desk is near the machine to remain alert and to tell you if the machine jams or stops before the copying is completed.
    c. Stand and talk with the coworker whose desk is near the machine so that you can hear if the machine malfunctions.
    d. Stand near the machine or use a nearby desk to complete minor tasks while you wait for the copying to be completed and listen for machine malfunctions.

Time-Wasting Incident 3

The company for which you work holds weekly meetings for all employees, but the company president rarely begins meetings on time. The meetings also usually run overtime, so the company holds the meetings before lunch and allows employees to take their full time for lunch and return at a later time than usual. You have found that these meetings interfere with your work schedule to the point that on meeting days you always have to stay after the close of the work day to complete tasks. What do you do?

    a. Take your lunch to the meetings and eat before the president calls the meeting to order or sit in the back and eat during the meeting, so that you can use your lunchtime to complete work.
    b. Second-guess how late the meeting will begin and work at your desk right until that time, then attend the meeting and take lunch as directed.
    c. Complain loudly to other employees that the president has an obligation to the company and to the employees to begin the meetings on time, making certain that appropriate executives hear your complaints.
    d. Save minor tasks, such as editing a letter or creating lists, and complete them during the time spent waiting for the meeting to begin.

Time-Wasting Incident 4

A coworker habitually stops by your desk on the way to the rest room, when going to the copy machine, and when going out to lunch and interrupts whatever you are doing with stories, gossip, and attempts to show you family photographs. You don't like the interruptions, and you don't particularly like your coworker, but you are determined to remain cordial because the company is small and you work in close quarters. What do you do?

    a. Put your head down and act as if you are deeply involved in your work while you ignore your coworker completely and make believe that you cannot hear or see anything but your work.

b. Bluntly tell your coworker to leave you alone and to go bother someone else with the nonsense from now on.
c. Smile nicely and pretend to be interested because you feel sorry for a person who seems to be so lonely and in need of attention.
d. Begin to complete one of several minor tasks that you have put aside on your desk, while you smile sweetly and explain, "I wish I could pay attention to what you are saying to (or showing) me, but I do have to complete this work before the end of the day."

Neither the incidents given as examples nor the range of reactions to each incident is unusual in a workday, but *how* we choose to deal with this lost time is unique to each person. Some people see peripheral time as downtime, during which they are not obligated to do anything more than wait for the action to begin once again. For others, such idle time is nerve-wracking and stressful, and it creates even more stress when the time wasted forces them to work after quitting time to make up for those lost moments.

How do you respond to each of the typical time-wasting incidents? Your reaction can have a great effect on how well you can become—and stay—organized at work.

HOW WOULD YOU DEAL WITH TIME-WASTING INCIDENTS?

Many tasks are too minor to warrant doing them during the regular workday, but they fit perfectly into the 5 or 10 minutes that we might wait during a telephone call or when a meeting begins late. To use this time effectively, however, you have to be able to put the tasks aside until peripheral time emerges, so any crucial task must be immediately ruled out.

How would you handle each of the time-wasting incidents? Would you try to complete minor tasks and, thus, eliminate the waste of time or would you bluster and try to move things along more quickly? If you selected **d** as your answer for the way to cope in all four time-wasting incidents, you have a good idea of how to become better organized at work. Let's review the choices and see what the professional pitfalls might be for some of the responses.

In Time-Wasting Incident 1, if you answered **a**, your actions would be useless. Most companies employ systems that answer calls in the order that they come in. Each time you redial, your call is treated as new and you are returned to the end of the list.

Choice **b** makes the caller appear to be foolish, if not hysterical, in attempting to place an order. In a rare instance, the operator might put you through directly to the sales representative, but that would be the last time, and you would be labeled a fool by the company. They will still take your money, but you might feel highly uncomfortable in future dealings.

Selecting **c** might seem to be a logical way to take your business elsewhere, but you must be careful not to rush off and strike up a relationship with an unreliable company. A long wait to place an order might be worthwhile, if the alternative is poor-quality goods, delivery problems, and a host of other problems that you might face.

Choice **d** allows you to express your feelings about the wait and to use the leverage that comes with the threat that a sale might be lost if this slowness of response continues. The threat seems more real if you present a calm, level-headed demeanor while indicating your displeasure. In addition, because you are ready for the wait and you have minor tasks to complete during that time, you do not experience the added anxiety of lost work time.

Answers to Time-Wasting Incident 2 offer similar choices for dealing with the problem. If you choose answer **a**, you risk an even greater loss of productivity than if you were to stand idly and watch the machine make copies. The copier may jam during the first few minutes of what you judge to be a 30-minute run, and you will not only have to then clear the machine of the jam but you will also have to make up for the 25 minutes of lost work time while the machine completes the run.

Selecting **b** takes unnecessary advantage of a coworker. A conscientious individual will sacrifice attention to work to monitor the performance of the copier for you, and that is not fair. In contrast, a person who will not allow anything to interfere with completing work might agree to your request, then completely ignore the copier and never notice if something should go wrong.

Choice **c** may make sense from your point of view, because you will take the responsibility of watching the machine for malfunctions. However, is it fair to your coworker whose work will be interrupted by your talking? Both of you will lose work time and probably have to work after quitting time to make up for the loss.

The most fair choice is **d**, because you can both complete work and allay your fears that the machine will malfunction. No one else has to experience interference, and the extra time that you have while the machine runs will allow you to complete small tasks that are usually put aside in the need to complete larger projects first.

Consider the solutions that are offered for Time-Wasting Incident 3. How comfortable would you be with choice **a** if you were in the middle of eating when the meeting began? If the company allows you to take the normal length lunch hour, eating lunch during the meeting is out of place.

Choice **b** is risky, because the meetings do not *always* begin late, although they may most of the time. If you choose to work up to the last moment before you believe that the meeting will begin, then rush in at the start of the meeting, *you* will appear to be late and disorganized. No positive result can occur, unless you know exactly when the meeting will begin and can manage to enter the room and be calmly seated before the president calls the group to order.

Selecting **c** will tarnish your image and make you unpopular with both your employer and with other employees. The president and other managers must be aware of the established time for the beginning of the meeting. If they choose to push the start later, they will not change their habits simply because you are making a loud noise. Instead, even those employees who may grumble in private will desert you and leave you to carry on your grumbling alone.

If you chose **d** as the best means of dealing with the incident, you have selected a way to continue completing work while you ensure that you will be on time for the start of the meeting, however late that may be. By planning slightly in advance, you can use the time to proofread or revise letters that you typed, to make lists of tasks for days ahead, to alphabetize items or the contents of files, or to perform a host of other tasks that don't require that you be seated at your desk. Lunch can wait until later, because the company is allowing you the usual amount of time, just in a different time slot.

Time-Wasting Incident 4 can influence your roles as both employee and coworker. Selecting answer **a** places a great strain on you and such behavior is even more cruel than simply telling off another person. Unless you have shown dissatisfaction before with your coworker's talking and interruptions, the stony silence and unresponsiveness will seem sudden and unexplainable.

Choice **b** at least establishes clearly that you are annoyed by the stories, gossip, and pictures. Stating bluntly that you can no longer stand to hear any more and that your coworker should bother someone else may be too candid. Do you really want to hurt someone's feelings—or is your goal simply to be allowed to do your work in your chosen time frame? If cruelty is not the aim, then you should consider another approach for dealing with this time waster.

In contrast to **b**, choice **c** is cruel to you. You may protect your coworker's feelings by smiling sweetly and pretending to listen, but eventually your guise will wear thin. The discovery at that time that you have been simply making believe that you are interested may be more difficult to deal with than if you were to cut off the flow of contact now. If you truly believe that the talking and need for attention are the result of a lonely life, you can show friendship in other ways that will not interfere with your work time.

Choice **d** is both the kindest and most honest way of eliminating the aggravation, and it should work for all but the most thick-headed of people. The reason that you should use the minor tasks to show how busy you are and avoid working on something that requires greater time and concentration is that the time spent waiting for your coworker to appear and to begin bothering you is truly peripheral time. You can't fully concentrate if you expect an interruption at any time, so you are wiser to complete a task that can be accomplished in a short space of time and that requires less concentration. You actually are working and you do not want to stay after quitting time, so you are not lying to your coworker. If you are busy each time that someone stops by your desk to annoy you, people will eventually understand your point. As you wait to make your point, put this peripheral time to good use by completing the brief tasks that often accumulate.

NEXT STEP

In this chapter, you have reviewed ways that you can become better organized at work by using time spent on hold for telephone calls or when waiting for meetings to start to complete minor tasks. In the next chapter, you will learn how to gain greater benefits from your use of the telephone.

CHAPTER 5

TURNING THE TELEPHONE INTO A TOOL

The telephone remains a necessary evil in a business world that thrives on instantaneous fax transmissions, global internet connections, and high-speed modem connections. Voice mail can only protect you from interruptions for a time—and answering machines only delay the inevitable. For most businesses, working the phones is the key to success or failure, so avoiding telephone contact is not an option. Why, then, does the telephone create such upheaval for many of us—and what can we do to make it work for us?

How you organize your telephone time depends on your job responsibilities and the freedom that you have to screen, accept, and reject calls. If someone else—a secretary or assistant—answers your telephone and screens your messages, you have the freedom to organize your telephone time according to your own priorities. If, however, you answer the telephone and must handle all complaints, requests, and demands voiced by callers, you are faced with the task of dealing with the telephone and with turning it into a useful tool.

HOW DO YOU USE TELEPHONE TIME?

The telephone can be a major obstacle to getting organized at work. It eats up valuable work time, whether we are making or returning calls. Nevertheless, unless we want to alienate clients and lose business, we can't just let the telephone ring or switch on the answering machine and selectively return calls. And, despite the e-mail explosion, the telephone is still a better tool for making a person-to-person contact when we can't personally meet with other people.

With planning and organization, however, you can make the telephone a valuable workday tool. To do so, you should be aware of how you use, or misuse, telephone time. Most of us blame the telephone and unwanted callers for the time that we waste on calls, but a lack of organizational skills could really be the culprit. You may be surprised to learn how much time you can save by simply organizing your telephone life.

Do you know your telephone IQ? Respond to the following questionnaire and find out.

Telephone IQ Test

Choose the response that best describes the way you would handle the following telephone tasks.

1. When I take telephone messages at work, I do the following:
    a. Ask for full information, including spelling of the caller's last name, telephone number, and best time for a return call.
    b. Tell the caller when to call back to reach the desired party, and post a message that the call came in.
    c. Leave a message that someone called and give the name and telephone number.
    d. Tell a coworker to remind me to tell the desired party that someone called.

2. I answer the telephone at work in the following manner:
    a. Identify the name of our company, then give my name and ask callers in a pleasant voice, "How may I help you?"
    b. Answer with the name of our company and ask, "What can I do for you?"
    c. Simply state the name of the company and wait for the caller to speak.
    d. Just answer "Hello."

3. To record telephone messages for myself and others, I do the following:
   a. Keep near the telephone several pens and a telephone message pad that has categories on which I can record the name of the person being called; my name; the date and time of the message; the caller's name, company, and telephone number; and a brief message.
   b. Use a legal pad on which I place relevant information.
   c. Write notes on plain paper and tape them to my telephone for later.
   d. Use the blank sides of envelopes to save paper and keep them in a pile on the corner of my desk.

4. When arranging a conference call for managers, I do the following:
   a. Call all participants to check their availability, set up a time for the call, then contact everyone involved and ask them to verify that they will participate.
   b. Poll participants to check their availability, then set up a time and inform all participants of the time.
   c. Set up a time for the call, then contact participants to verify their participation.
   d. Set up a time for the call and send participants notification of the time.

5. If I must put a caller on hold, I do the following:
   a. Ask the caller, "May I put you on hold?" then wait for an answer and check in every 30 seconds or so to remind the caller that I have not forgotten.
   b. Ask the caller if I may put him or her on hold and wait for an answer, but not waste my time checking.
   c. Simply warn the caller, "I am going to have to put you on hold."
   d. Not say anything, and just put the caller on hold since I have to do so anyway.

6. If my company upgraded the telephone system and made substantial changes, I would do the following:
   a. Ask to be given specific training and instructions, so that I would be familiar with all the changes.
   b. Request an instruction booklet or sheet to keep near my telephone for ready reference.
   c. Ask coworkers to provide a summary of the changes and new features.
   d. Learn as I use the new features and, when I make mistakes, explain to callers that the system is new.

7. If my company has had several recent problems and angry people are calling to voice their complaints, I would do the following:
   a. Ask my supervisor to instruct me how to respond to the callers and to whom the complaint calls should be directed.
   b. Ask the callers to specify their complaints, take down the information, and give the information to my supervisor.
   c. Tell callers that they are not alone and that a lot of other people have also called with the same complaints.
   d. Tell callers that there is nothing I can do.

8. If my coworkers ask me to take telephone messages for them when they are out to lunch or taking a break, I would do the following:
   a. Take a message as accurately as possible if the occurrence is rare, but warn coworkers that I will not spare the time if too many calls come in.
   b. Take messages when it is convenient, but not antagonize coworkers with any warnings.
   c. Tell my supervisor that coworkers are wasting my time with their personal requests.
   d. Simply ignore the telephone when others are not in the office.

9. If my boss asks me to screen calls and say that she is not in the office, I would do the following:
   a. Ask her what she specifically wants me to say and to tell me if I should lie to everyone who calls or just to specific callers.
   b. Modify the response to callers and say that my boss is not currently able to talk with them.
   c. Feel uncomfortable and say that I have been told that my boss is not available.
   d. Simply ignore callers' remarks and tell them to call back later.

10. If I have to make a business call to someone with whom I am not familiar, I do the following:
    a. Get organized before the call and write a brief agenda that contains the main ideas of what I want to discuss.
    b. List my main points of discussion on index cards for reference during the conversation.
    c. Make the call and see in which direction the conversation goes.
    d. Let the other person do most of the talking.

Now compute your telephone organizational skills IQ score. Give yourself 5 for every **a** response, 4 points for every **b** response, 3 points for every **c** response, and 1 point for every **d** response.

Scores from **41** to **50** show a high degree of organization in telephone skills. You have a logical and orderly approach to dealing with telephone tasks, and you are able to control the unexpected and sometimes unpleasant tasks demanded of you by others.

Scores from **31** to **40** show a strong awareness of necessary telephone organizational skills but less use of them. You seem to know what you must do to organize your telephone activities, but you are less likely to take the same approach every time. You probably modify the way that you handle a situation, depending on the caller.

Scores from **21** to **30** indicate a tendency to be disorganized, although you can certainly improve with the right structure and tools. You may find that making lists and sticking to them will eliminate some of your telephone troubles.

Scores from **11** to **20** mean that you really have to take stock of your situation. Start with the simplest of solutions and build from there. Organize yourself before making or taking a call, and keep materials available with which to take notes so that you cannot procrastinate in taking and giving messages. Later in this chapter you will find valuable suggestions in the "Telephone Top Ten" for increasing your telephone IQ.

HOW CAN YOU AVOID TELEPHONE TAG?

The single most frustrating time waster about telephone communication is the not-so-pleasant game of telephone tag that we are forced to play. The game comes about in various ways: Someone calls you while you are out, busy with another call, or involved in a meeting or an important task. Your assistant or a coworker takes the call and dutifully writes down the name of the caller, the time that the call came in, the telephone number for you to return the call, and the message, if any. When you return to your desk, depending on your work load, you return the call and find that you must now leave a message. The game may continue for days, with both callers missing each other and leaving messages that do nothing more than build up frustrations and leave you wondering why somebody doesn't just write an old-fashioned letter and end this silly game of tag.

The results are not much better if your caller and you both have voice mail—unless you rewrite the rules of telephone tag and create a strategy that works. What would you do if you were in the following situation?

Situation 3

Jan is the office manager in a physicians' practice that has two sites and contains four physicians and five office assistants. Two of the office assistants are responsible for answering the telephone and for taking messages for the medical and office staff. As manager, Jan oversees the daily operations of both office sites and must frequently drive from one to the other with reports, copies of files, and other materials that must be hand-delivered. Calls from suppliers and other businesses or from patients with billing questions are handled by Jan, who is often in transit. When returning a call, Jan frequently finds that the caller is unavailable, and thus begins a very frustrating game of telephone tag. Which of the following would you do to eliminate this problem?

   a. The medical practice should acquire a cellular phone for Jan to carry when traveling between office sites, so that calls can be returned immediately.
   b. Jan should be assigned a specific voice mailbox on the office telephone system to expedite easy access from any site and for more rapid return of calls.
   c. The office assistants should be trained to take *complete* messages that will save both Jan and the caller time in their attempts to speak with each other.
   d. Jan should leave complete information with people at both of the office sites, so that callers will know when to expect a return call or when Jan will be available to receive another call.

Solution **a** *seems* to be the easiest, because Jan can simply use a cellular phone and return calls as they come in. Easy? Perhaps. Efficient? Not at all. Even if the cell phone has caller ID so that Jan can screen calls and avoid time wasters, calls from suppliers and patients usually require access to purchasing or billing records or to other materials that are only contained in one of the office sites. The only response that Jan might give when answering the phone while in transit is a promise to locate the needed information and to call back as soon as an answer is available. Such a response does not usually satisfy a caller who has made verbal contact and expects results *now*.

Solution **b** places more control in Jan's hands and serves as a screening process to allow for a quick return of calls that require simple answers and a delay for other calls that require research. The hazard here is that the caller may be unavailable, and Jan's return call will simply be the second step in what might become a lengthy game of telephone tag.

Solution **c** provides a more valuable approach that will save time and eliminate aggravation for Jan. The key to making this solution successful lies in defining what constitutes complete information. The person who takes a call for Jan should not merely ask, "Any message?" A more organized approach is needed. The office assistant should ask the caller to clearly specify the following information:

1. the caller's name with correct spelling
2. the reason for the call
3. what action the caller wants the person called to take
4. the time when the caller is available for a call back
5. the telephone number where the caller may be reached during the specific time

Callers may become annoyed at having to provide such detailed information, but answering these questions provides benefits to both the caller and to the person called. If you know that someone is only available during a specific time, then neither party will have to waste time playing telephone tag.

Solution **d** is also valuable and should be combined with **c** to allow both callers and Jan the maximum opportunity to connect with each other. Callers who do not receive a return call within an hour or two often call back repeatedly, wasting office staff time *and* becoming angrier with each repeat call. If they are informed of Jan's availability when they call the first time, they will know to wait for a time before feeling snubbed. Of course, some people refuse to believe what they are told and will insist on calling back at regular intervals, no matter how much information they are given.

HOW CAN THE "TELEPHONE TOP TEN" ORGANIZE YOU?

Make the telephone your most useful tool by controlling when and how you use it. Not all calls must be returned immediately, so wait until you are ready to devote a block of time to returning *important* but not *critical* telephone calls. You might also decide that some calls do not even warrant a response. Plan to become as efficient with your telephone time as you seek to become in other areas of your professional life. The following suggestions will work for you.

The Telephone "Top Ten"

1. **Create a directory** of the most important telephone and fax numbers that you call and keep it next to your telephone for ready reference. This list should contain not only important clients and other business contacts, but should also include technical support numbers for vital office equipment.
2. **Establish a specific time** in the day when you return telephone calls that are not of an emergency nature. Grouping calls in this manner allows you to create blocks of uninterrupted work time and to control the amount of time that you spend—and waste—talking on the telephone.
3. **Cut down on telephone tag** by telling callers or leaving messages on their voice mail that indicate a specific time that you will return their calls. Making telephone appointments in this manner cuts down on the need for others to call you at times when you are out. Formalizing an intended call by setting a time also makes others more likely to wait for your call, thus lessening the possibility that a flurry of telephone calls will result.
4. **Return calls** that do not require extensive explanations during times when the recipient is likely to be out of the office or about to leave. If your call is simply a brief response to a question, or if you have only a brief question to ask, call right before or during lunchtime or just before the end of the workday. Most people will not want to talk with you for too long at these times, and you will obtain even more direct responses than if you called earlier in the day and became bogged down in a lengthy conversation.
5. **Return calls** that require lengthy explanations via e-mail or fax to avoid misunderstandings. Let the recipient know that you are responding through one of these means and your reason for doing so. Because lengthy information may often have significant consequences, and because responses to such information may take up too much of your time, request that others respond to you via e-mail or fax. Remind people that this arrangement permits you both to have a hard copy for future reference.
6. **Leave complete messages** on answering machines or voice mail when you respond to calls or try to connect with another person. In addition to your name, telephone number, and the time of the call, leave a message that includes a time when you can be reached by telephone. If your call is to obtain information, provide your listener with your complete question and all the specific details, so that you will receive a complete answer from your respondent.

7. **If you use voice mail** or an answering machine, write down detailed information as you listen to each message and delete the messages immediately. Saving the messages to listen to later seems like an efficient idea, but it can backfire when you accumulate too many messages. A backlog on your answering machine will slow you down as you waste time scrolling through old messages to arrive at the new ones. Voice mail is less aggravating, but hearing "You have 20 saved messages" should hardly make you feel efficient and organized.
8. **Prioritize the information** in long telephone calls, and cover the most important issues first in case the call is unexpectedly cut short. Because you might feel harried or hurried when you have numerous points to cover in a telephone conversation, organize your thoughts on paper and create an agenda before making an important call. As each point is covered to your satisfaction, cross it off the agenda and move on to your next point.
9. **Provide the recipient of your call** with full information at the outset, so that you will either receive needed information or your call can be transferred to the right person to help you. At least give your name and affiliation, as well as the reason for your call. By stating, "Hello. This is Clark Kent of *The Daily Planet*, and I'm calling to speak with the person in charge of your line of superhero uniforms," you provide the call recipient with enough information to decide where the call should be transferred.
10. **Use a telephone headset** for your workday calls if you take a lot of calls or if you must complete other tasks while speaking on the telephone. Instead of twisting your head and neck to jam the telephone receiver between your shoulder and ear, you can move about freely while you sort mail and papers, clear the desk, or take notes as you listen to the caller.

The "Telephone Top Ten" provides a practical approach to taking control of the telephone and turning it into a tool that will help you get organized at work. You have to be firm with callers and make them understand that your time is valuable and, although you value their calls, what they have to say cannot be permitted to interfere with your productivity. As you practice your new approaches to using the telephone, you will find that you will become more organized in other areas as well.

NEXT STEP

In this chapter, you have learned ways that your telephone can become a useful tool, instead of a source of frustration. In the next chapter, you will find valuable tips for identifying hidden time wasters and learn how to discourage people politely from wasting your valuable work time through socializing.

CHAPTER 6

FOCUSING ON PROFESSIONAL, NOT SOCIAL, TASKS

People are harder to reorganize than inanimate objects. Move a chair or a bookcase to just the right spot, and it will remain there until moved by you or by someone else. The same cannot be said about people.

Don't expect coworkers, contacts, or superiors to remain at a distance or to allow you time to complete tasks, because they won't—unless you establish clear ground rules. Ideally, coworkers should see that you are busy and they should refrain from interrupting you with tales of their latest social disasters, but don't count on that. If you rely on blind trust here, your efforts to work will be largely unsuccessful.

Socializing in the office and on the telephone consumes a lot of time that would be better spent in completing work. Why stay an extra 15 minutes or half hour to make up for time lost when you stared with glazed eyes at pictures of a coworker's recent vacation or listened to someone's latest tale of woe? Why not simply identify the ways you can organize the people in your life—and spend your work time on professional instead of social tasks?

WHY WON'T PEOPLE SIMPLY LET YOU WORK?

Have you noticed that people will interrupt during your busiest moments or at crucial points in a project? At least, this always seems to be the case. You wonder how they could not know how busy you are, while they wonder why you are fuming. As you try to continue working and ignore the interruption, the person tries even harder to gain your attention and you try even harder to keep working. Feelings are hurt and tensions rise, and you find yourself even more distracted than if you had simply allowed the interruption in the first place.

The solution is not to accept all interruptions as inevitable. Instead, you have to turn these enemies of your time into allies. To do that, you must let people know what you are doing and how they can help.

Your past socializing has set a pattern for your coworkers, and you cannot blame them for expecting you to continue in your old ways. If you have always been a ready listener, quick to drop anything to empathize with a coworker's latest plight or to compliment pictures of a new addition to someone's family, then you have set a pattern of behavior that they have every right to expect until you change those expectations.

What does this mean for you? Unless you clearly tell others that you are focusing more on the job and less on social interaction, they will probably not notice. And those that do notice may misunderstand and stop speaking to you because their feelings will be hurt and you will seem to be snubbing them.

Have you any idea how much time socializing wastes in your workday? Most likely not, because those isolated minutes seem insignificant on their own, but they add up to large blocks of time over a day or week. If you really want to organize how you spend your time in the office, you have to know how you *waste* time as well as how you *spend* time.

To learn how much time you spend socializing, you will need to use two tools: the "Time Assessment Survey" that appears in Chapter 3 and the "Social Time Wasters' Dirty Dozen" found on the next page. You may be surprised by your answers to both measures.

Use the "Time Assessment Survey" and keep a time assessment log for one workweek. Make certain to include in your log the names of all people with whom you socialize in the course of each day. Once you have completed the log, you will use it to examine your time use carefully and thereby learn where you can gain extra minutes in a day and extra hours during the week. Your responses will also help you to identify the people who are wasting your time, so that you can plan strategies for making them your time allies.

> ## Social Time Wasters' Dirty Dozen
>
> Place an "X" next to those behaviors that describe the ways you waste time at work by initiating the action. Place an "O" next to those behaviors in which coworkers waste your time by initiating the action. If you *and* your coworkers are guilty, place both letters on the line.
>
> ____ Showing photographs taken during a recent vacation or family event.
> ____ Passing around photographs of a child, grandchild, puppy, or kitten acting cute.
> ____ Relating the minute details of a new romance, down to the wine served at dinner.
> ____ Regaling others with accounts of past jobs and experiences, or those yet to come.
> ____ Complaining about office conditions or the way workers are treated.
> ____ Asking for or giving directions at every step in routine projects that have been repeatedly assigned.
> ____ Placing or receiving non-work-related telephone calls that can wait until after work.
> ____ Relating personal family incidents and problems in detail.
> ____ Discussing vacation plans and looking at travel brochures.
> ____ Discussing the merits of restaurants in the area while planning lunch.
> ____ Stopping to receive status reports on family or romantic problems.
> ____ Stretching lunch or breaks by starting a few minutes early or ending a few minutes late.

The "Social Time Wasters' Dirty Dozen" contains some common social time wasters. Use it to identify the people who are the major time wasters in your work life. Of which time-wasting behaviors are your coworkers or supervisors guilty? Of which are *you* guilty? Do you waste your own and other people's time in any of the following ways? Combined with the time assessment log, you will also identify the amount of time that you can save each day just by avoiding certain situations, or by modifying your own behavior.

How much of a social time waster are you? To answer that question, review again your responses to the "Time Assessment Survey." Then, do the following:

- Make a list of the types of socializing that you and your coworkers did during the week that you assessed.
- Add the number of minutes for *each* type of incident to see how much time you spent in a week looking at coworkers' pictures, complaining about your job, or making personal calls—no matter who initiated the behavior.
- Place the number on the line following each example of social time-wasting behavior in the "Social Time Wasters' Dirty Dozen."
- Add the number of minutes spent on each item to see how much time you spend socializing during a workweek.
- Are you surprised by what you learn about the time that you spend socializing during one week? For a more specific view of this time, answer the following questions and place the appropriate numbers on the lines following each question.
- How much lost time per week is your fault? ____ minutes
- How much lost time per week is the fault of others? ____ minutes
- Who *are* those others? ____ coworker ____ boss ____ client ____ supplier ____ mail carrier ____ other (_____)

To see how this assessment can help you organize your work environment, consider the case of Ryan, an employee of a car dealership.

Situation 4

A bookkeeper and cashier in the auto parts sales department of a busy car dealership, Ryan is surrounded by distractions. Coworkers and customers always seem to have something to say to her, and the telephone rings continuously. She also answers the telephone as part of her job, and she finds that even unknown callers tend to become friendly and waste her time by talking about subjects that are unrelated to auto parts. Maintaining good customer relations is important to the image of the dealership, so Ryan cannot hang up abruptly and continue working. She must also deal in a friendly manner with people who buy auto parts, even if their conversation tends to wander. Such interruptions result in a substantial amount of time spent socializing, and this time is increased through interruptions by coworkers and personal calls. On most afternoons, Ryan stays almost an hour after the parts department closes to enter transactions into the computer and to tabulate the purchases and sales of the day.

Ryan kept a "Time Assessment Survey" log for a week and found that she had wasted almost a full workday in socializing during that week. She then completed the "Social Time Wasters' Dirty Dozen" to identify the time wasters and the total time spent socializing during her week, as well as those who initiated the socializing. Ryan's responses to the second measure appear below.

The total time that Ryan has spent socializing during a week totals 325 minutes—a total of 5 hours and 25 minutes that could otherwise be spent in produc-

---

Social Time Wasters' Dirty Dozen: Ryan

_O_ Showing photographs taken during a recent vacation or family event. 10 min.—boss

_O_ Passing around photographs of a child, grandchild, puppy, or kitten acting cute. 10 min.—customer 1; 15 min—customer 2

_O_ Relating the minute details of a new romance, down to the wine served at dinner. 15 min.—coworker 1; 10 min.—coworker 2; 5 min.—coworker 3; 15 min.—customer 1; 10 min.—customer 2

_O_ Regaling others with accounts of past jobs and experiences, or those yet to come. 15 min.—coworker; 10 min.—customer

_O_ Complaining about office conditions or the way workers are treated. 10 min.—coworker 1; 15 min.—coworker 2; 10 min.—coworker 3

_X O_ Asking for or giving directions at every step in routine projects that have been repeatedly assigned. 10 min.—Ryan; 25 min.—coworker

_O_ Placing or receiving non-work-related telephone calls that can wait until after work. 15 min.—coworker

_X O_ Relating personal family incidents and problems in detail. 5 min.—Ryan; 20 min.—coworker

_X_ Discussing vacation plans and looking at travel brochures. 10 min.—Ryan

_X O_ Discussing the merits of restaurants in the area while planning lunch. 15 min.—Ryan; 20 min.—coworkers

_X O_ Stopping to receive status reports on family or romantic problems. 5 min.—boss; 10 min.—Ryan; 15 min.—coworker

_X O_ Stretching lunch or breaks by starting a few minutes early or ending a few minutes late. 15 min.—Ryan; 10 min.—coworker

tive work. Furthermore, because the average loss of time each day is more than an hour, if Ryan would spend this time completing her work, she could probably leave on time each day as soon as the department closes.

Does *your* workweek contain the same periods of time wasted in socializing? If it does, you can eliminate them by changing the way the people who surround you at work view you and by making them understand that you need to focus on professional, not social, tasks. This won't be easy, and doing so without hurting the feelings of others or alienating coworkers and friends can be tricky—but it can be done.

CAN YOU GAIN TIME WITHOUT LOSING FRIENDS?

Before you can succeed in reorganizing the people with whom you work, you have to begin with an image makeover for yourself. Your biggest task in turning social time into professional time may lie in changing the perceptions that others have of you.

Take a look at the different ways that Ryan initiates socializing during the workday. Coworkers see that in one week she initiated discussion about personal family incidents and problems, discussed restaurants and vacation plans, stopped to receive status reports about their family or romantic problems, and stretched her breaks and lunchtime. In short, Ryan initiated 65 minutes of socializing. Given her actions, can her coworkers be blamed for assuming that she is just as willing to join them when they also initiate socializing? Their assumptions are justified because of her behavior, which has created an image in their minds that will be hard to erase.

In addition, Ryan has always politely listened to her coworkers when they have told her their problems, shown her their pictures, and complained to her about their latest fiasco in the office and their feelings toward their jobs. If being polite has ever made you sit with glazed eyes as people pulled out one photograph after another or related a seemingly endless list of details, you may have also fooled others into believing that you welcome such behavior. Inside, however, you may have been silently screaming with frustration, hoping to end the socializing and return to work, so that you could end your day on time. Why didn't you? Were you afraid of being rude? Were you afraid that you would hurt someone's feelings?

Such concerns are admirable in most social situations, but not at work. Although you may feel pressured to join others around the water cooler or at the coffee machine, you must remind yourself that these activities will not help you complete your work. Getting organized at work means using your time to attain maximum efficiency, not becoming the most popular person in the room.

So how can you make others understand and accept your new goals? Start with yourself. Review the assessments and identify the areas in which you have sacrificed work time for social time. Examine each incident carefully and try to remember how that lost time interfered with your workday and prevented you from enjoying personal time.

- Did you have to stay later just to complete work?
- Did you take shortcuts that lessened the quality of your work?
- Did you feel frazzled? Stressed out?
- Was the time spent socializing important?
- What effect did the lost time have on your feeling of control over your work?
- What effect did the lost time have on the extent to which you felt you had control over your life?

Once you know when and where you are most likely to become distracted, plan to remain alert to those situations. First of all, you will have to convince your coworkers that the change in your attitude toward work is serious and permanent. This may be hard, because people are creatures of habit and they may have some difficulty accepting the change, especially because they may begin to feel guilty about their own behavior at work. Some might feel that you are being unfriendly, and others might even feel insulted.

What you do about these reactions depends on how important various people are to your life. Do not mistake this for license to be rude. Instead, you should assess your relationships and divide your coworkers into categories, according to their importance to your life. Three possible categories follow: (1) people whom you genuinely like and with whom you have developed an emotional relationship; (2) people whom you like but who have little or no impact on your life; and (3) people whom you can gladly do without.

Focus on maintaining a solid work relationship with people in categories 1 and 2, and use your newfound dedication to organizing your life at work to eliminate the people in the third category. Let the people who count know what you are doing. You must communicate your goals if you expect their cooperation, because so great a change in your work habits is sure to be confusing. Your boss should also be considered in the second category, because most superiors at work have an effect on our lives.

Finding the words to let others know that you have changed is not as hard as you might think. Be honest. If you are tired of rushing through your work and of leaving long after the day should end, say so. If you have an especially stressful project due, or if you feel that your work performance has held you back from promotions, admit this as well. Once your coworkers know that you have specific goals, they will be less likely to take your new behavior personally. In fact, you might be surprised to see how supportive they will be of your efforts.

Not everyone, however, will applaud your change of heart. In attempting to communicate clearly your goal to work rather than socialize, you should also be ready to meet resistance. Such resistance might simply be the result of others' desires to continue a friendly relationship with you and not a deliberate attempt to sabotage your new effectiveness. In this case, be kind but firm in dealing with the person who interferes with your organization of time. Offer options for socializing during lunch or after work, but do not let sympathy for a coworker's problems or repeated dilemmas keep you from proceeding with your newly developed sense of organization at work.

NEXT STEP

In this chapter, you focused your attention on dealing with the situations and people that lead you to waste time in socializing rather than working. The next chapter will show you how to manage your tasks effectively and to use no more time than is necessary to complete your work.

CHAPTER 7

MANAGING TASKS EFFECTIVELY

Many people who work for others tend to feel that they have no role in arranging the time and the order in which they complete certain jobs. All they know is that certain tasks have to be done on a daily, weekly, or monthly basis, and those tasks had better be completed on time or their jobs will be in jeopardy.

Have you ever felt that way about a continuing responsibility or an ongoing project at work? No matter how high your position in a company, someone else with greater seniority always exists—and you may feel that you are being continuously scrutinized. You may also feel that your supervisor controls when and how you complete your assigned tasks, but that is not necessarily true, and you should not allow it to be true. More than you realize, you *do* have the power of creating priorities—and of deciding how to fulfill those priorities.

Work must be done, of course, and you must meet certain schedules. However, as long as your work is thorough and completed on time, you should do your work in the manner that makes you feel most in control. You can take control of your job by allocating and investing your time and resources wisely, and managing your tasks effectively.

HOW DO YOU TAKE CONTROL?

Before you can take control of your tasks, you should clearly identify them and establish if they must be completed on a daily, weekly, or monthly basis. Knowing what to do and when to do it provides you with a framework for getting organized at work.

What are your duties? Check all of the following duties for which you have either total or partial responsibility.

Task Management Checklist

____ Opening the mail for everyone in the office.
____ Distributing the mail.
____ Typing purchase orders or bills of lading.
____ Typing correspondence, including letters or memoranda.
____ Preparing reports.
____ Retrieving and sorting overnight fax messages.
____ Distributing overnight fax messages.
____ Answering and redirecting all incoming telephone calls.
____ Taking telephone orders.
____ Typing order sheets for telephone purchases.
____ Filing incoming correspondence.
____ Filing library or reference information.
____ Filing archival material.
____ Clipping newspaper and magazine articles on designated topics.
____ Retrieving and sorting overnight e-mail messages.
____ Distributing overnight e-mail messages.
____ Photocopying documents.
____ Preparing outgoing mail.
____ Maintaining an inventory list of supplies.
____ Ordering supplies.
____ Preparing checks to pay bills.
____ Maintaining employee health insurance records.

____ Maintaining employee payroll records.
____ Preparing payroll checks.
____ Making client contact calls.
____ Monitoring workday e-mail messages.
____ Monitoring workday fax messages.
____ Other _____
____ Other _____

Are you surprised at how much you actually do? If you are employed by a large company that has many employees, your tasks are probably less diverse than someone who works in a small company in which employees must wear multiple hats. In a large company, however, whereas the variety of tasks will be less, your involvement in each will be more intense.

Review the list and determine how you can create task categories. Grouping tasks can increase your feeling of control over your work because doing similar tasks within the same time period will allow you to focus your energy on one area. This approach is also valuable in helping you to avoid the types of errors that result from trying to work on too many types of task at once. By focusing your attention on one category of task, you will also reduce the frustration and fragmentation that many of us feel when we must simultaneously give our maximum effort to several areas.

The number and nature of your duties will determine the categories that you create. As the Task Management Checklist suggests, if you are an administrative assistant in a large company in which strict categories of work obligations are maintained, you might have four daily duties that solely relate to typing. You might be a paralegal responsible for research, investigation, and administration, or a bookkeeper placed in charge of employee records. The majority of us have several duties to perform each day, and some may have to deal regularly with 20 of the 27 listed duties.

What is your situation? How can you manage your duties better? Consider grouping your tasks into one or more of the following categories: typing, telephone calls, reading and reviewing, mail management, and personnel chores.

Do not make the categories too narrow by ignoring the many ways in which various tasks are connected. For example, your tasks may include sorting and distributing incoming mail, and you may also be responsible for retrieving and distributing fax and e-mail messages received overnight when the office is closed. Why not sort and distribute the three types of messages at the same time? Alert your office manager or other supervisor that you are doing so. Then coordinate your retrieval times for the mail and fax and e-mail messages. Let everyone know that you will give them all three types of messages at the same time. Not only will you save time and effort, but others will also benefit because they will receive all incoming information at the same time.

This approach works just as well regarding other tasks. Categorizing duties has many benefits. You will save time by combining duties, and you will also gain a greater control over your tasks as you become increasingly adept at identifying similarities and eliminating unnecessary steps and effort. You can only do so, however, if you take time to plan and to schedule your work.

WHAT'S YOUR PLAN?

To get organized at work, you have to both *plan* and *schedule* your tasks. Bear in mind the difference between these two actions: When you plan, you decide *what* you will do; when you schedule, you decide *when* you will do what you have planned.

Take the time to plan your tasks, even if you have orders from supervisors to carry out set duties each day. If you are a manager, you should make planning an integral part of your management style and encourage employees to plan.

Don't just look at your daily tasks when planning. Take a longer view by also developing realistic weekly and monthly plans. Many of us have weekly or monthly tasks, in addition to those that must be completed daily, but we tend to ignore them and various meetings or appointments when planning because they happen with less regularity. Don't make this mistake.

Plan both your long-term and short-term tasks. List your small tasks and place approximate times for their completion in parentheses next to the task. "Filing" alone sounds intimidating, but when you identify the type of filing, such as "filing reference articles," you make the task seem more concrete and more reasonable to complete.

In contrast, long-term projects should take up more space in the planner and more of your planning time. Do not just note the deadline of the final project. Instead, as soon as you are given a long-term project, break it into manageable parts and begin to schedule the time to complete each segment.

Create a rough breakdown of the project, listing all the steps from beginning to end. Estimate the time needed for you to complete each step and make certain that you are overly generous with yourself in determining how long each step will take to complete. Identify a start date and a completion date for each step, and enter these dates on the planner calendar. At the same time, identify the information and materials that you will need to complete each step. You should also decide on the concrete actions that you have to take to complete each step.

Your planning materials don't have to be elaborate. You can use something as simple as a ring binder with dividers to create sections for calendar sheets that have daily, weekly, and monthly capability; address and telephone number sheets; and appointment sheets. On the other hand, you may choose one of several elaborate personal planning systems, such as DayRunner, Running Mate, Franklin Quest, Filofax, and Week-at-a-Glance.

Keep either a planner or a week-at-a-glance calendar on your desk with your usual daily and weekly schedule clearly noted. Update the planner as additions and changes are made to your tasks and add reminders as they become necessary for one-time tasks. You should also consolidate the changes and additions each day and place them in a logbook or section of the planner to provide yourself with a record of continuing projects and completed tasks.

Many of us fall into the habit of tacking and taping scraps of paper containing important information to a bulletin board, the computer, the desk, or the wall. These pieces of paper are easily lost, and the search for missing information can waste precious hours. Why chance that? By using a planner, you will not only eliminate playing hide-and-seek with paper, but you won't have to face recreating vital information from memory when the papers can't be found.

"Tickler" files should be included in the planner. Such files may be nothing more than separate folders or envelopes, one marked for each day of the coming month, into which you may place notes regarding conversations, special instructions, or items related to meetings or projects scheduled for that day.

Paper planners are very popular, but the computerized personal information manager (PIM) is growing in use. You can use a PIM to prioritize your to-do list, schedule meetings, track telephone calls, store notes, and remind you of appointments. The information can be accessed quickly and accurately.

Can you use a PIM? Your answer depends on both your current job responsibilities and on your career goals for the near future. A well-organized employee usually gains positive attention, and positive notice increases your chances for advancement. Why not use every reasonable tool to aid you in projecting the right image at work?

PIMs are of two types: contact managers and task managers. Both types include a calendar with daily, weekly, and monthly capabilities; to-do list makers;

address books; and appointment schedulers. If your job involves significant client contact and interaction with people outside your company, you will probably find the PIM contact manager more valuable. This type of PIM is ideal for sales teams or consultants who might have to negotiate a project to its end. They are also handy for documenting calls, faxes, and letters that relate to a specific project.

In contrast, the PIM task manager focuses on scheduling and it is most useful for people who have to work on projects that have distinct tasks and deadlines. This type of PIM allows you to record the assignment of certain tasks to specific people and to collect material from several sources. You will find the task manager PIM particularly valuable if you work on several projects at the same time, because it can show the progress of each task within individual projects. Some task managers have the capability to connect contacts with tasks or to arrange tasks into an outline or a list. If you feel that a PIM would be helpful to manage your tasks, make certain that the to-do list of the model you choose allows you to set priorities and due dates.

Whether you choose a paper or an electronic planner to help you get organized at work, you should also create a file that tells where other important information can be located. The type and extent of this information depends on your areas of job responsibility. Make certain to include an updated list of important names and telephone numbers, a clearly explained list of your office procedures, equipment information (including make, model, serial number, and warranty information), and an alphabetized list of the files contained in the cabinets that you maintain. Place these files in a locked drawer for your own reference and for others who are authorized to possess such information, should you be out of the office for an extended period of time. Compiling such information in advance will also save you substantial stress should you need to locate any of it in a hurry.

WHAT ARE YOUR TASK PRIORITIES?

As you plan and schedule, you will also have to set priorities among your tasks. Bosses and deadlines may appear to establish your priorities, but you have a lot more freedom than you might imagine in determining which tasks are most important and which can be put aside or completed later.

Use your planner to identify your priorities. Begin with a weekly plan that identifies all long-term and ongoing projects in which you are involved. Identify first the projects that you feel must be completed, then list the remaining projects in decreasing order of importance. In the daily sections, schedule time for your daily tasks, such as typing memos, sorting and distributing mail, and others that you may have checked in the Task Management Checklist. If you call for supplies weekly, pencil in that task on the appropriate day. If you type up the monthly report during the last two days of the month, pencil in that task. Include in the planner all meetings, tasks, and other actions that take up your time on a regular basis. Then pencil in other tasks and appointments as they occur.

Once you have a written plan, stick to it and don't let anyone convince you to deviate from the plan without *very* good reason. If you usually call the office supply company on Friday morning at 10 a.m. to order material for the following week and a coworker stops at your desk to talk just as you are dialing the telephone, tell the person to return later. Once you have identified your pattern, maintain it. Consistency plays a big role in achieving success in your effort to manage your tasks.

Physical organization is also important to managing tasks. Consider how this is true in regard to paying bills, one of several duties that you might have.

Should bills be paid at a regular time each month, or should they be paid as soon as they arrive in the office? Scheduled bill paying as opposed to paying bills on demand allows you to deal with one task on a set basis and reduces the possibility of errors. You should have everything that you need in one place to complete the task efficiently and quickly: envelopes, checkbook, a tray for receipts from paid bills, stamps or postage machine. As bills arrive in the mail, open them and mark the exact due date and the amount on the front of the envelope. Put a note on the calendar to pay any bills that cannot wait until your regular bill-paying day, or make a list of bills as they come in and place an asterisk next to those that require special treatment. As you make out the checks, place a mark next to the appropriate bill on the list and be careful to enter the check number, date, and amount paid in the check register.

Many businesses enter this information into duplicate records to protect important financial information. Others do not. The same diversity exists among when companies choose to pay their bills. Whether the company that employs you requires that you pay bills on demand or on a scheduled basis will depend on the nature of its business and business transactions. If no preference exists, choose the organizational approach that works best for you.

Now apply the task management techniques to managing the mail. For many of us, sorting and distributing the mail is a routine exercise. We look at the recipient's name, alphabetize our piles, and give the mail to the appropriate people. In some cases, the "appropriate" person is your boss, but in other cases it is you. Consider how you might manage the task of sorting and distributing the mail if your boss has asked you to save what is only important.

Situation 5

Aaron is an administrative assistant in an insurance agency. His boss has asked that Aaron give him only personally addressed letters. He has also told Aaron to refrain from giving him any of the 10 magazines to which he holds subscriptions. Instead, Aaron has been instructed to remove articles related to topics that the boss is interested in knowing or learning about and to place them in reference files. These are not Aaron's only duties, but he accepts them because he is working toward a promotion and wants to show that he is a well-organized employee who can easily manage any task given to him. How does he accomplish this task?

Aaron's Solution

Aaron knows that he has to be selective in deciding what is important enough for his boss to read, but he can't take a chance of throwing away an important letter or a journal that contains a significant article. So he has created a list to identify what will go into the trash can and what will travel to his boss's desk.

Aaron opens the mail each day, keeping nearby a tray marked "To Read" and the trash can for discards. He places in the "To Read" tray only typed or handwritten envelopes addressed to his boss and those containing specific names of companies or individuals in the return address. He throws away all advertising and solicitations, as well as any mail addressed only to "Occupant" or "Business Owner."

To help him decide which articles to save, Aaron has created a precise list of the topics in which his boss is interested and he modifies the list as he finds that some of his choices are rejected. When magazines arrive during the week, Aaron puts them into a special tray then waits until Friday and spends about an hour each week reviewing the magazines, removing articles, and filing the articles in the reference files. He used to review the magazines as they came in, but none arrived on some days, while several arrived on other days, and the time spent reviewing articles disrupted his ability to complete other tasks. He has been more successful now that he schedules a specific time each week for the task. To determine if an article is appropriate, Aaron first scans the table of contents of a magazine and circles the page numbers of possibilities. He then reads the lead and the concluding paragraphs of the article to see if the title is accurate. When he first began this task, many articles fooled him because their titles sometimes promised something entirely different from the discussion in the article.

If an article is appropriate, Aaron carefully removes it from the magazine, neatly writes bibliographic information at the bottom of the first page, and stacks the article in the "Library File" basket. After going through all the magazines, he binds the discards for recycling, then separates the articles and files them in the reference files. With his boss's agreement, Aaron does not remove articles that are more than 10 pages long. Instead, he neatly prints a large index card with the author, title of the article, title of the magazine, volume number, month and year, and page numbers, and files the card in the appropriate reference file folder for later retrieval from a library or data bank.

Newspaper articles pose another problem. The paper is fragile, the text wears off, and folding long article pages often obscures important words. Thus, Aaron makes photocopies of the articles, taking care to reduce page size so that the copy fits neatly into the reference file folders.

NEXT STEP

You have identified approaches to managing your tasks more effectively. The next chapter will show you how to organize your desk area to achieve maximum work efficiency.

SECTION III

ORGANIZING YOUR DESK ENVIRONMENT

One of the most annoying statements of all time is also one of the most important rules to follow in getting organized at work: "A place for everything and everything in its place."

You will feel more in control of your work if you are in control of your work environment—and for most workers "environment" means the desk and surrounding area. You will save time and also project a competent image if you can immediately locate whatever you need without having to first restack papers, move stacks of folders, or search through every drawer in the desk.

The chapters in this section will guide you in organizing your desk environment and help you to create a place for everything that you need to get organized at work.

CHAPTER 8

ARRANGING YOUR DESK LOCATION

Think of your desk and the area surrounding it as your home away from home, which it is for about eight hours each workday. You may not find it as inviting as home, because you are not permitted to relax comfortably and put your feet up as you wish. Yet, in the same way that your home defines you personally in the eyes of others, the desk area defines you professionally.

The ideal workstation is the right size desk located in a well-lighted, quiet area of the office—near all of the necessary equipment but well away from the major traffic. Unfortunately, unlike the personal comfort decisions that we are able to make at home, the work environment does not always permit employees to make many choices of accommodations in the office.

The location of your desk is important to your success at work, but the amount of control that you have in this area varies from company to company. Even if you do not control *where* your desk is located, you might find means of improving the situation in other ways. Through simple planning and organizing, you can create a more comfortable desk area that will increase your work efficiency and make your work environment personally more pleasant.

IS YOUR DESK A MAGNET FOR DISTRACTIONS?

The location of your desk plays a major role in the amount of work that you complete and the quality of that work. A desk near the rest room and the coffee machine might seem ideal and convenient, but it is also in the path of heavy traffic. In this situation, even your best intentions to keep working and to ignore the people who pass will not help you to maintain the careful concentration that your work requires.

The conversations of others, the movement to and from the rest room and coffee machine, the sounds of doors opening and closing, and everything else suggested by the location will grate on your nerves. Even if coworkers go about their business and do not stop to speak with you, the sound of their talking and their actions will still have a negative effect on your productivity and will defeat your best efforts.

Is the location of your desk a problem? To answer that question honestly, pretend that you are a visitor who is not familiar with either the daily operation of the office nor with your tasks and abilities as an employee. What would that visitor see when she looked at the location of your desk? How many of the following are characteristic of your situation? Place a check next to all of the statements to which you can honestly answer "Yes."

_____ Are people constantly walking past or around your desk?
_____ Is the desk near an entrance or exit?
_____ Is the copy machine or another high-use piece of equipment located near the desk?
_____ Is the desk located near windows that contain large and noisy air conditioning units?
_____ Is the supply cabinet located near the desk?
_____ Are file cabinets that are used by the entire office located near the desk?
_____ Is the lighting inadequate for you to work comfortably at the desk?
_____ Are electric outlets inconveniently placed, thus preventing you from adding a desk or floor lamp?
_____ Is the desk near a radiator or in-floor heat register?

____ Is your access to the telephone limited because of an inconveniently located telephone jack?
____ Is the desk the wrong height to allow you to compose work comfortably on the computer?
____ Is the desk the wrong height for you to rest your arms while doing hand-written work?
____ Is the desk too small to contain the office equipment that you must use, i.e., computer, telephone, electric pencil sharpener, mail opener, fax machine?
____ Is the chair too high or too low for you to sit comfortably while working at the desk?
____ Is the chair too heavy or hard to move easily away from the desk?

How does your desk space rate? To determine this, count the number of items that you checked above. Each can be a source of discomfort as you attempt to work. If you combine several of these distractions, then you have a situation that can seriously hamper your ability to work efficiently.

If none of the above items is checked, enjoy your office environment because your work situation is rare and you are a very fortunate employee. Most of us who work for others have several reasons to complain about the setting in which we work, because we have not had any role in its planning.

If you checked from 1 to 5 of the items, you may be able to function after exerting a great deal of self-control, but you should take steps to make changes wherever you can. The energy and effort that you are forced to use in dealing with these discomforts would be better spent in focusing on your work tasks.

Did you check from 6 to 10 items? If so, you are really fighting an uphill battle trying to work under such conditions, and you have every right to bring this issue up with your boss. How can you function efficiently under such uncomfortable and unbearable conditions? You shouldn't have to, and a company that values you as an employee must take measures to eliminate at least some of the problems. The key to achieving change is your manner of approaching the people who can best effect such change. An example of the correct approach appears later in this chapter.

If you checked 11 or more items, you do not need to be told that your situation is very difficult and that accomplishing work of any value is relatively close to impossible. You are also probably feeling a great deal of stress, the result of trying to complete your assigned work while having to cope with so many negative environmental factors.

If you share an office or work in a company that has many office workers, then you probably feel that you have little control over where your desk is located. That may be true, but you should try to change the situation anyway. You might find that no one has ever tried because they have felt that no one would listen, so no changes in location have been made in the past. That doesn't mean that change can't occur now.

HOW CAN YOU IMPROVE YOUR SURROUNDINGS?

The key to changing the location of your desk and your comfort levels lies not in complaining but in providing an alternative plan. Although the desire to feel more comfortable while you work is enough reason for *you*, a boss will want to know how this change will be beneficial to the company. So, be prepared with a well-supported argument before you ask anyone for help.

You will achieve more positive results if you follow these steps:

- Review your list of dissatisfactions carefully.
- Decide what is most difficult for you to cope with and, thus, most important for you to change.
- Identify how that change would increase your work efficiency while it also benefits the company.
- Package your request for a change in location or an improvement over your current situation in a way that shows a result in benefits for your company.
- Submit your concerns to your immediate supervisor as a request for help and not as a means of confrontation.

Consider how Jayne used this approach to improve her situation soon after she was hired and realized the negative effect that an uncomfortable and noisy location had on her productivity. What would you do in her situation?

Situation 6

Hired by a large and successful catering company to maintain the computerized financial records, Jayne was given a desk near the elevator along an interior wall that contained a large number of electric outlets. Her supervisor suggested that Jayne would probably appreciate the arrangement because equipment in addition to the computer would later be added to her desk. Although the beautifully maintained, old-fashioned oak desk and chair were highly attractive, their heights were not suited to working at a computer and they could not be adjusted.

In addition, the opening and closing of the elevator doors and the voices of people entering and leaving the elevator interrupted Jayne's concentration and led her to make several potentially serious errors. What seemed like a series of isolated problems finally led Jayne to realize that she was being hampered by the location of her desk and that something had to be done about her situation if she were to achieve maximum efficiency. The desk telephone rang while she was working on a spreadsheet that tracked the company's yearly profits. As she reached to the far end of the desk to answer the phone, located there because of a distantly placed outlet, she accidentally pressed against the keyboard. The screen went blank, and work that had taken her hours to enter just disappeared.

What would you do if you were in Jayne's situation? As a new employee, she was hesitant about drawing attention to herself, yet the mistakes that might occur due to her uncomfortable desk location could result in her being fired. The temptation was strong for Jayne simply to remain quiet about her situation and to bear with the noise and confusion until she felt more secure with the company. After the telephone disaster, however, she realized that she would be wasting valuable time if she continued simply to adapt to the situation and did not seek change. She decided to take a chance.

Jayne's Solution

Rather than run immediately to her supervisor and discuss what had just happened to her big project, Jayne reasoned that she should first redo the project then present her case when submitting the project results. She knew that her work was good, and presenting concrete evidence of her value to the company while asking for concessions seemed to make more sense than just demanding change.

Jayne first made a list that identified the problems existing with her current desk environment, including the location too close to the elevator, the noise and distractions of the human traffic, the incorrect height of the desk, the uncomfortable chair, and the difficult access to the telephone. She explained how these problems had interfered with her earlier work and used the profit report as her primary example, then asked that several modifications be made to help her to achieve maximum work efficiency. Jayne gave both her written request for the change of location and the completed profit report to her supervisor at the same time. She noted clearly on a separate sheet of paper attached to the report why it was delayed and what simple measures would prevent similar mishaps in the future.

After reviewing the report, Jayne's boss spoke with her and, with the cooperation of several others in the company, ordered maintenance people to move Jayne's workstation to a quieter area with a closer telephone outlet. To provide a lower desk surface to hold the computer, the company purchased an inexpensive desk extension that was lower than the height of the desk. Jayne purchased a leather-look cushion to make the chair more comfortable. To compensate for the needed electric outlets, Jayne bought a heavy-duty power strip, for which the company reimbursed her. The move provided an unexpected benefit, because the new site was along an exterior wall near a window with a pleasant view.

The solutions to Jayne's problems may not work for everyone because all companies do not have the room to relocate employees and their desks, and additional outlets may not be available. Perhaps your problems are different and require more creative means to solve. Let's address other problems, such as noise, light, and temperature.

Your desk may be situated near the photocopier, and you may have to deal with both the talking of your coworkers and the constant noise of the copier. Depending on your daily tasks, you have a variety of ways to deal with the problem if your desk must stay put.

- If copying noise interferes with your work, review your schedule to see if you can rearrange tasks to create a large block of time when you can perform tasks away from your desk. Then speak with your supervisor and ask if large copying jobs can be blocked into that time frame. You can't prevent the emergency run of three or four copies, but even this concession will provide benefits.
- Ask a supervisor if you can use an empty office or other space to complete work that requires your devoted attention. This request is also a diplomatic way of alerting others to the negative effects of the copier noise.
- If no other solution is available, use earplugs to block out the noise. You may feel foolish at first, but your coworkers will soon understand.

Is the light around your desk too bright—or not bright enough? In some offices the sunlight pours in through the windows, providing discomfort to those seated in its direct path. In other offices, the bulbs used in light fixtures and lamps are of too high wattage, and the resulting glare makes reading at the desk difficult.

- If natural light is the problem and you are seated near the windows, close the shades or blinds to block the light. Offer to trade desks for a time with coworkers who protest that they want the sunshine to continue to stream in.
- If high-watt light bulbs are the problem, ask if bulbs of lower wattage can be substituted in light fixtures. Change the bulbs yourself in desk or floor lamps.
- Reposition your desk chair or desk if the light falls in the wrong place of your work area.
- If existing light is insufficient, ask if you can bring in a desk lamp or, if floor space is adequate, a floor lamp.

Is your desk area too warm—or too cold? Even with the pleasure of central heating, corners of large rooms and areas near the windows may feel too cool for comfort.

- Ask if you can move your desk out of a draft or nearer to a heat vent. If a lack of space prevents this, ask if you may bring in a personal electric space heater to place under your desk. For your safety and that of your coworkers, make certain that the model you buy meets government safety standards.
- If your work area is too warm, ask if you may bring in a small box or oscillating fan. Make certain that the fan is aimed at you and that it does not blow the papers off the desks of your coworkers.

Can you do anything to organize your access to the telephone better if an outlet is too far from the desk?

- If the distance to the outlet means that your desk telephone must be placed dangerously near the edge of your desk or on an inconvenient-to-reach corner, simply purchase a longer modular plug cord to connect the telephone to the wall outlet. Be careful to avoid leaving loose wires where people walk. Either attach the telephone wire to the baseboard with lightweight U-tacks or use clear packaging tape to hold the wire down.

- If you are not permitted to add a longer wire, ask if you can have a small table on which to place the telephone safely, to avoid accidents. You might also use a rolling cart that can provide additional shelf storage.

A well-organized desk environment has a positive effect on how we complete our work because it makes us feel good about our surroundings. Just as important is the organization of the desktop, over which we have control of what appears and how these items are arranged.

NEXT STEP

In this chapter, you examined some approaches to arranging and organizing your desk location. You will now take a critical look at your desk and decide how you must organize it so that you can work smarter.

CHAPTER | 9

ORGANIZING YOUR DESK

Are you tired of making excuses for your messy desk and of struggling to find telephone numbers, files, correspondence, or even your telephone under the piles of paper that have accumulated on your desktop? When was the last time you could immediately put your hands on a pencil or pen when you wanted to jot down a telephone number or address quickly? Have you avoided opening one or more desk drawers because you fear finding the decomposing remains of a leftover sandwich from lunch last week?

You may have decided that you have no problem as long as the drawers of your desk stay closed, but this cannot continue. Once the clutter in your desk has forced you to spend more than a few seconds to locate a needed item in a drawer, the time has come to clean your desk. Not just the desktop that others see, but every drawer and the area surrounding the desk, as well.

WHY WORRY ABOUT WHAT IS ON YOUR DESK?

The condition of your desktop is important because it is another means by which others judge your competence as an employee. The time that you spend hunting for papers and supplies is wasted time for your employer, as well as for you. While you are frantically pawing through a drawer looking for an important file, your boss may be doing a slow burn as she waits. Depending on the nature of your job and responsibilities, your desk may also be a vital element in the way that others judge your capabilities. You may protest that you are able to find everything needed, but a cluttered desk often sends a negative signal to others, who see the disorganization as the sign of a disorganized individual. Don't just shrug off such concerns—take action. Others may decide *where* your desk is located, but you can control *how* the items and materials that you need are arranged.

As you look at the pile of clutter on your desk, do you have a difficult time imagining what you can do without? While on your desk, everything there may seem necessary and irreplaceable, but it contains a large number of items that you can live without. You will find a lot to throw out once you begin to scrutinize the piles of papers and boxes of half-used supplies that accumulate so easily in a short time.

As with any major project, you should plan your approach before cleaning the desk. Before you begin weeding out items, obtain three boxes to contain the papers and files that you remove from the desk. You should also place an empty trash can near the desk to encourage you to throw out useless paper and other items, rather than keep them and return them to their former places.

To organize the desktop successfully, you must start with a clean desk surface on which to work. You will have this if you begin by clearing everything off the desk—all papers, files, supplies, and equipment—then place them on the floor at a distance from the desk, so that you don't add to the chaos. If you place the piles too close to the desk, they will be in your way and will add to your cleaning frustration as they fall and papers scatter.

Because you plan to be thorough, take everything out of the desk drawers and separate all papers from the rest of the items. You will sort and file these papers with the piles of paper that you took from the desktop. As for the remaining items from the desk, put your tools, supplies, and personal items off to the side for later sorting, because you will first focus on organizing the paper.

Once the desk has been emptied, clean every inch of it so that you can organize a truly clear desk. Start with the desktop and use a slightly moistened cloth to remove all dust, coffee stains, glue marks, and anything else that has spilled onto or stuck to the surface. Are you unsure that this is necessary? You should view what you are doing as marking a new beginning, because it is. Not only are you making an important effort aimed at getting organized at work, but this also means taking a new approach to your work habits. If you are extending your efforts to your desk, why not start fresh with it, as well? The desk may have never been this clean, even when you first sat at it, but the effort to not only *clear* the surface but to also *clean* it has special significance. In taking the desk back to its almost-new state, you are also emphasizing your commitment to make a new beginning.

Treat your desk as if it is a valued element in your working life. If your desk has a solid wood or a wood veneer surface, polish it with a spray wax to complete your preparations. If the surface is metal, use a metal polish.

Now, you are ready to begin the work of organizing your desk materials, but leave the papers for later. Handle and scrutinize everything that you removed from the desk. Ask yourself the following questions about each item and decide what absolutely must be on the desktop.

- Do I need this item to complete tasks?
- How often will I use it?
- How will I use it?
- Do I have another item that can do this task and others, as well?

As you carefully make your decisions, return necessary items to the desktop one by one, and evaluate the need for each item individually.

The single most important item among such essentials is your computer or typewriter, which should occupy a central position on the desk unless you have been provided with a separate workstation or an adjustable desk extension for it. First position the computer or typewriter in a suitable place on the desk, then replace the other desktop items in a logical manner. You might also place the telephone and a message pad next to each other on the desk, making certain that the telephone cord is not too taut and the telephone is easy to reach. Boxes labeled "IN" and "OUT," a desk calendar, and a rotary address file should also have their places in the desktop. Rather than leaving it lying as an open file on the desk, place your current project in a box labeled "PENDING."

You should also have second thoughts about some items. Many people also choose to keep a framed personal photograph of family, friends, or pets on the desktop to remind them of their lives outside the office. Doing so is a personal decision, but you should give careful thought to the nature of the photograph and whether or not your work situation makes doing so wise. Do you really want strangers who enter the office to see so personal an aspect of your life?

Whether the photograph is of you, your family, or your dog, consider the following discussion that took place between Gina, a doctor's office assistant, and Jim, a pharmaceuticals salesman, after he showed an interest in the photograph of her daughter dressed in a rhinestone-covered costume at a ballet recital.

Situation 7

As he waited for Gina's boss, Jim made idle conversation while he looked with boredom around her small office. Catching sight of her daughter's photograph, Jim complimented Gina for having "a cute little girl." After she thanked Jim, he picked up the framed photograph and talked for a few minutes more about how quickly girls grow up today and how dangerous the world is for young children. Even though his manner remained pleasant, Gina became uncomfortable with his focus on her daughter and she waited nervously until her boss was free.

After Jim left, Gina slipped the photograph into her purse and vowed not to return it to the desk. When she later thought about the conversation, she could not explain what exactly had upset her, yet she knew that something had made her uncomfortable about Jim entering her personal life by discussing the photograph.

Gina had no way of knowing that Jim had recently had his own moment of difficulty because of the family photographs that he used to keep on his desk. His experience reveals another reason why many people refrain from keeping personal photographs on their desks in view of others—their fear of not being taken seriously.

Jim is usually on the road for most of every day, but he returns to the pharmaceuticals company each afternoon to inventory his samples and to prepare activity reports for the day. For months, he had kept several framed photographs of his wife and children on his desk. He recently took them home after his boss looked at a newly added family group photograph and commented loudly to several other salesmen, "Looks like Jim here is the only person in the company with some family values—and he sure proves it."

The comment might have been made in a joking manner, but, real or imagined, Jim had sensed an edge to his boss's voice, which signaled danger. Knowing that the company values team players who are willing to work long hours for the company, he did not want to lose the opportunity for a promotion on the chance that management thought that he was too distracted by family matters. His accumulation of family photographs was unusual when compared to the impersonal-looking desks of his male coworkers, so Jim simply decided to conform to their approach.

Are Gina and Jim being overly cautious and alarmists? Perhaps they are, but neither has any way of knowing who will see their photographs and what the result will be. Your good judgment must prevail, and you should seriously question if personal photographs on your desk are revealing far more than you intend.

WHICH PAPERS SHOULD YOU KEEP?

After you have returned all necessary items to the desktop, begin the real work of sorting through the papers and file folders. You have already placed "IN," "OUT," and "PENDING" boxes on the desk, but don't use them immediately. Instead, begin by sorting the papers into three piles, one containing papers that you will file, a second for papers that you will discard, and a third for papers that fit into neither category and which must be given further consideration. Move the trash can a little closer and begin the laborious task of deciding which papers stay and which must go.

To be most effective at this point, handle and look at every sheet or scrap of paper that originally occupied the desk. You will be more selective in choosing how much you will keep if you view each piece of paper as an individual decision to be made. More clutter remains when you review paper in clusters, because simply transferring stacks of paper from one spot to another does not require the same careful decision making. As a result, this action also doesn't give you enough reason to discard.

Now is the time to make some hard decisions and to send into the trash any paper that is not necessary to keep or to consider further. Before you do, record in the appropriate place any information of value that appears on a paper.

Below is a guide to how you should handle items that are not directly linked to your work.

- Personally interesting articles or notes don't belong on your desktop, so either throw them into the trash can or take them home.
- Scraps of paper containing personal or work-related telephone numbers, addresses, or reminders should be entered into the appropriate address books or planners and then thrown out.
- Reminders of personal and professional appointments should be recorded in a planner and then thrown out.

- Labels, advertisements torn from newspapers or magazines, and directions for after-work activities should be taken home or thrown out.
- Invitations to professional events should be recorded in the planner then thrown out.
- Invitations to personal events should be taken home and recorded then thrown out.
- Thank-you notes should be thrown out.

Use the above list as your guide to handling all paper and deciding whether to keep it.

After you have sorted all the papers, you will have two stacks, those to be filed and those requiring further sorting and consideration. Put the second pile aside and work on the papers to be filed.

File these papers into one of the three boxes on your desk. Place information entering the office into the "IN" box, and place material that should leave the desk via filing, mail, or being passed on to a colleague into the "OUT" box. Use the "PENDING" box for material that represents work in progress or that requires further information.

These three boxes can be valuable tools in your crusade to achieve paper control on the desktop, if you use them right. Sorting every paper that comes to your desk will keep you organized, but don't allow the boxes simply to become depositories of clutter.

- Items that are placed into the "OUT" box during the day should leave the box by the end of the day. Because such items are either filed or sent by mail, keep sheets of letterhead, envelopes, and postage or the postage meter near the "OUT" box to ease the process of emptying it.
- Items in the "PENDING" box should only remain there for a short time, while awaiting further action. Don't use this box as a dumping ground for items that you don't know what to do with.
- Items in the "IN" box should be relocated by the end of each day. Place completed items into the "OUT" box to mail, file, or give to someone else to process. Deal with everything in the "IN" box each day, and do not allow items to pile up.

Review all the papers in the second pile that put you put aside and try to sort them as well. Many may go into the trash, now that you have given them a second review, but others will probably be passed on to someone more appropriate to process. After the desktop is clear, organize your desk drawers and be as severe in throwing out unneeded and unwanted material as you were in sorting the paper. First prepare the desk. Use a plastic desk tray to separate items and to provide order in the drawers. Install trays or bins to hold pencils, pens, paper clips, a ruler, scissors, markers, bottles of correction fluid, a stapler, and staples. As you return items to the desk, eliminate duplication of supplies. You don't need to be a pack rat because the office supply cabinet should contain the quantities of supplies that you need. Return the duplicates that you find to the supply cabinet. The same is true for other supplies that you are tempted to hoard. The only exception to this caution is in regard to supplies that you use extensively on a daily basis and which you might run out of.

You can also keep needed personal items in the desk. Use one of the smallest drawers to hold only those that you might need during the day, but don't turn it into a junk drawer.

ORGANIZING YOUR DESK ZONE

After returning necessary items to the desktop and the desk drawers, you might still have boxes of materials around the desk. Difficult as it is, you have to apply the same principles of organization to these items that you applied to materials that you removed from the desk.

Ruthlessly sort through the accumulated items and dispose of all unnecessary paper and supplies, then prepare to file or find new areas of storage for remaining paper and supplies. Now organize the desk zone so that all frequently used equipment and materials are within arm's reach.

To determine where to place such items as the fax machine, telephone book, reference binders, office supplies, and file cabinets, take the following desk zone test. Sit in your desk chair and spread your arms in all directions while you remain seated.

Can you reach everything you need while remaining seated? If not, consider ways you can rearrange your desk zone to provide additional surfaces on which to place items that you need to reach.

- Reposition the desk at a different angle to change the distance from your chair to important items.
- Place a small bookcase butted against the side of the desk to store software manuals, reference binders, and reference books. Arrange the manuals

according to their category or project or develop another system, and label the categories in large type.
- Place the file cabinet within reach of your desk if you are the only person who uses it, so that you will more readily return materials to their folders.
- Move the fax machine, printer, telephone, and answering machine to tables or stands within arm's reach.
- Obtain a rolling cart to carry frequently moved supplies and files and keep it at arm's reach.

As you make the desk zone a more convenient place to work, you can also make it more comfortable for yourself. Purchase such inexpensive comfort accessories as a wrist pad for the computer to relieve the strain on your wrists. Place an antiglare screen on the computer monitor to alleviate eyestrain and an antistatic mat beneath your chair and feet. Bring in a footrest to prevent leg fatigue and to make yourself physically more comfortable. Before you bring in personal items, check with a supervisor because some companies may have office rules against doing so.

Organizing your desk area is not only beneficial to your state of mind, but it may also be beneficial to your career. When bosses need specific information, they are more impressed with someone who can locate relevant data within a short time than with the person who claims to have a complete report filled with statistics on the issue but cannot find it. An organized desk also looks good—and it makes *you* look good, as well, because you appear to have mastered your environment rather than remained at its mercy.

NEXT STEP

You have reviewed various ways to organize your desk and to create order in your desk area. The next chapter will guide you in creating a more efficient filing system to help you organize information and locate it quickly.

CHAPTER 10

ORGANIZING YOUR FILES

The best system of organization is one that is consistent in all areas and clear to all employees of an office. If you and others in the office must share files, contact names, supplies, or other items, then everyone should have the necessary information to understand *what* the system contains and *how* it works.

Filing is a key activity in any system of organization in a business because an accurate system of record keeping is usually the backbone of business operations. Information about past, present, and future activities is kept in company files—on paper, disk, or hard drive—and knowing what type of information is available as well as the correct means of accessing that information is vital to success. If you're not convinced that this is true, imagine what might happen if an important letter or contract that you have recently filed could not be located. Would your company lose an important sale? Might it be subject to a lawsuit? Would people lose their jobs? All of these results are possible. With a good system, however, such potential disasters are preventable.

The focus of this chapter is to examine ways you can organize the many types of information and services that exist within a company. The goal is to help you create approaches that will increase your effectiveness and cut down on your frustrations.

WHAT IS YOUR FILING SYSTEM?

You probably inherited a filing system when you were hired because most companies set up some form of system early in their existence. Bills have to be paid, correspondence is sent and received, and tax records accumulate. These items have to be placed somewhere, and that somewhere is usually the start of a filing system.

As you have probably already learned, not all filing systems are equally effective. Many new employees of seemingly well-established companies have been shocked by the disarray in which they find the company files. Even more shocking is that they are expected to maneuver through the files and continue to maintain order in a chaotic system. Shauna found this situation when she began working as the sole office employee in a small but successful art gallery.

Situation 8

Shauna knew that she would be receptionist, file clerk, and everything else when she took the job as an administrative assistant in a successful art gallery. The pay was good, and she enjoyed the thrill of meeting new and established artists who were friends of the gallery owners.

She had expected to work hard and to stay late on most nights. What she had not expected was what she found the first time that she attempted to file the seemingly endless stacks of papers that had accumulated since her predecessor had been fired. The four-drawer file cabinet looked neat enough from the outside, but the mess inside was obvious to Shauna as soon as she opened a drawer.

Papers had been randomly stuffed into folders, some files were alphabetically arranged and others were numerically arranged, and archive, reference, and active files were mixed together. Faced with such confusion, Shauna wondered how the gallery had become so successful. Because she would have to file the papers that were overflowing the two "OUT" baskets on the desk, she decided to create a filing system suited to the needs of the gallery before she did anything else.

Could you be faced with a similar problem if you changed jobs? Are you now facing this situation? Your filing system might not be so badly organized, but you probably would prefer that it were better organized.

The first step to identifying the best filing system for your company is understanding the types of files that are common to all effective systems. Every filing system should contain files that fall into three broad categories:

- working files that must be kept close at hand
- secondary files to which you refer only periodically and which can be less accessible
- archive files which can be stored out of the office and are only rarely referred to

Working files are active files that contain information that you need *now*. They should be placed in a file cabinet that is readily accessible to you; the cabinet should preferably be located at arm's reach. Client accounts, expenses, personnel records, transactions, and the like all belong in the active file. You add to active files daily as you sort and file incoming mail and bills, and you will probably keep much of the information contained in these files. What you will purge will be duplicate invoices, letters, or other items, and unnecessary files.

Reference files are also current, but they consist of information that might prove useful as research or support information. They do not contain material that refers to the daily operation of the office. You should scrutinize these files more harshly and purge them more freely than you do the working files.

Keep the following guidelines in mind when reviewing reference files:

- Ask yourself under what circumstances you would use the information. If you can't think of any reason to keep the material, throw it out.
- If you decide to keep the information, decide which key words would come to mind if you wanted to locate it. Consider *how* you will use the material as your way of determining the appropriate key words to use.
- If you are filing items of the same type, such as fax or copier manuals, place the material in the broader category file ("Manuals"). Then place a note in the specific equipment type file ("Fax" and "Copier") to indicate that the specific manual appears in the general category file "Manuals."
- Use cross references as they are needed.

Archive files usually contain information and documentation that remains from completed projects or accounts that are no longer active. Laws and policies vary as to how long to keep records, and many companies that have substantial storage space simply keep everything from their first days of operation. Other companies purge their archive files on a regular basis because of space limitations, and they keep only legally required documents.

Review your company's policy to learn how long you are expected to keep specific types of files. Also refer to Chapters 18 and 19 of this book for general guidelines.

Even if the records are no longer active, you should periodically go through the archived files to see if you can combine materials and organize the files to make them even more efficient. In some cases, the reactivation of an old account requires that you locate archived files and place them in the active or working files.

Even if archived files are long since inactive, don't just dump a large amount of related papers into one folder. Instead, divide broad topics into new, more clearly defined categories. As an example, you might take the five-inch-thick copier file and divide it into subjects according to brand, financial arrangement (buy or lease), type (high volume/full feature), or whatever else works. As with active files, check all the folders and merge all related files as you throw away duplicate items.

IS THERE A BEST WAY TO FILE?

The best way to prepare to structure your filing system is first to become familiar with the mechanics of organizing files. You might do this either when first setting up a new filing system or when organizing an old and inefficient system after unnecessary items have been purged. You may have inherited a filing system that has "always" been used in the company, but if you feel that you can do better with a different approach, the company will be better off, and so will you. Don't continue to lumber along with an inefficient system. If you do, your productivity will eventually suffer, and valuable material is certain to be misplaced or lost. Instead, approach your boss with suggestions for changing the old system. Arm yourself with a list of reasons why the present system is undesirable to continue and provide alternatives to the current approach.

Your choices are limited as to the overall type of filing system you can use because only two basic systems exist: alphabetical or numerical. Fortunately, within these two broad categories exist many ways you can personalize your system to fully meet the needs of your company. The geographical location of the company by which you are employed, the product or service marketed, the nature of its business transactions, and volume of business all determine which system is most appropriate to use. And they all may affect the specific structure of the system that you develop.

Numerical Filing System

The numerical method is less frequently used, so let's deal with that first. If your company business is technology related or if dates hold a high priority, a numerical system might be relevant to your filing system. The manner in which this method is developed may vary from company to company, but most numerical filing systems use one of three general organizing approaches:

- Consecutive numbers in which files begin with "1" and advance by one as each new file is created, e.g., 00001, 00002, . . ., 99999.
- Coded numbers in which files begin with the lowest number of the code set, i.e., student identification numbers, then advance as new numbers are assigned. The last two digits of the year may be used as the first two digits for the coding. Following is an example of one approach to coding, using the year 1995: 950001, 950002, . . ., 959999.
- Chronological file numbers in which 12 main categories, representing the months of the year, are created then file folders numbering 1 through 31, representing the days of the month, are included in each of the 12 categories, e.g., 1–1, 1–2, . . ., 12–30, 12–31.

In organizing the files, don't feel that your company must conform to one of the above examples of numerical filing systems. Instead, study the business transactions that are most common to your company and devise a filing system that meets those needs.

Does your company manufacture and distribute a range of products, each carrying a different product serial number? Develop a system to capitalize on this. Rather than grouping files according to a general numerical system, you might find that your system will be more effective if you organize the files according to the product serial numbers.

If you work for an insurance agency, you might find that combining the alphabetical system with the numerical system would provide the most logical and comprehensive filing system. The names of policy owners are best served by alphabetizing, but using policy numbers as a means of organizing files is especially useful in making policy and client information readily available to agents.

Is the company that you work for service-based? If it is, the filing system will benefit if you apply the numerical system to organizing their files according to invoice number. Number and letter prefixes and suffixes provide additional divisions within file categories, and additional information appears in alphabetically arranged cross-referenced files.

To devise an effective filing system, remember that one approach does not fit all companies. The key to effectively using a numerical filing system is to create a structure that reflects the characteristics of your company.

Alphabetical Filing System

More common is the alphabetical method, which is a bit more complicated than it might appear at first glance. We all learn the alphabet in kindergarten, but alphabetizing files requires that you know more than your ABCs. Most companies that use the alphabetical approach modify the method to suit their needs because they must do so to make it work well. In addition to simply running through the alphabet, you might also have to devise categories and then alphabetize the files according to city, state, or country; company name; subject of the files; product type or name; or last name of key individuals. Whichever approach to customizing you choose, make certain that it is determined by the needs of your company. You will find that simply taking a generic system and attempting to impose it on your company will not provide the most efficient system.

Despite the differences in methods that companies might use, all types of alphabetical filing systems follow several important rules of organization:

- File documents according to the first letter of the first main word, and place "the," "a," and "an" after the main words, e.g., "James Company, The" and "Little Flower, A."
- File documents according to the last names of people, and place such titles as "Mr.," "Ms.," or "Dr." after the name, as appropriate or needed, e.g., "Arnold, Sean (Ms.)," and "Asky, Dean (Dr.)."
- When the first letters are the same, go to the second letter to determine alphabetical order. If the first two letters are the same, go to the third or the fourth, as needed, e.g., Deanen, Deanne, Dear, Deer.

- Think of abbreviations as they exist in their spelled-out form and file documents accordingly, e.g., "St. Paul" precedes "Saint Peter"
- File companies according to their *exact* spelling, e.g., "Toys for Us" precedes "Toys Я Us."
- File compound names according to the names and ignore the conjunctions, e.g., "Aaron Properties" precedes "Aaron and Ragson"
- File digits according to their spelled-out form, e.g., "10 Club, The" precedes "Tragar's Gym."
- File government documents according to the most important division and use the subdivision to qualify the category, e.g., "United States Congress, House Ways and Means Committee" precedes "United States Congress, Transportation Committee."

HOW CAN YOU MAINTAIN YOUR SYSTEM?

Once you have selected a filing system and organized your file folders, take a little more time to organize what is placed in those folders. The few minutes that you spend in giving attention to these organizational tasks will provide long-term benefits in the amount of time that you will save and the aggravation you will avoid later. Whether your file organization is alphabetical or numerical, you will reap important benefits by doing the following:

- File only what you *really* need to keep.
- Remove paper clips from all papers because they create bulk in the folder if they stay on or accumulate at the bottom of the folder if they fall off.
- Staple related pages of a single document, so that the entire letter or report will be viewed and individual pages will not be misfiled.
- Check already stapled documents before filing to make certain that the pages really do belong together.
- Arrange single sheets and stapled documents within a folder in reverse chronological order, placing the most recent first.

No matter what organizational approach you use, you should periodically go through all of the active files in each drawer of the file cabinet, vertical file, and desk drawer file. By doing so, you can make certain that the headings are still current and useful, and that the contents of the folders are up to date.

Do you have a file maintenance plan? Do you schedule the cleaning of files on a regular basis? You should. How often you do so depends on the size of the company you work for and how busy the office is.

Organizing files is not an easy task, and it may take a complete day or more, even in a small company. A larger company conducts more business and records more transactions, so the files are more numerous, and organization becomes a greater chore. If the number of files is too great to go through in one day, divide the files into manageable batches. How you divide the files into these smaller batches will depend on the structure of the current filing system. Below are some suggestions:

- Chronologically arranged files might be divided based on a set number of years. For example, you might decide to review one year of files at a time or, if the files are less numerous, five years at a time.
- Alphabetically arranged files could be divided according to a range of letters of the alphabet. Depending upon the thickness of the files, you might choose to review from **A** to **C**, **D** to **F**, and so on. If each file is very thick, you might decide to complete the review of one letter of the alphabet daily.
- Numerically arranged files might be categorized by blocks consisting of a certain number of files in number order. For example, you might begin at the beginning and review the first 50 or so files, from 00001 through 00050, and so on.

However different the means by which you categorize the files, to make the task manageable, you have to take the same methodical approach to organizing and purging all three types of file organization systems. In essence, you should follow the approach that you would use in cleaning and organizing the papers on your desktop. In this task, however, the papers have already been filed, so they should be divided into only two categories: "Refile" or "Discard." As you sort through the files, be thorough and remember that the work you do now will make your daily filing much easier.

NEXT STEP

This chapter has reviewed various approaches to creating an efficient filing system that will suit your company's needs. In the next chapter, you will learn ways you can use color coding and visual elements to make effective connections between tasks.

CHAPTER | 11

USING COLOR CODING TO GET ORGANIZED

Has all this talk of taming time, purging paper, and managing materials made you even more reluctant to tackle the tasks that will help you to get organized at work? Does all of it seem to be just a little too much work with no fun attached?

Well, it may be true that getting organized is not fun, but you can make it a little more pleasant and a lot more effective. How? By adding color and visual aids to the solid plans for organization that you have already identified.

WOULD YOUR FILES BENEFIT FROM COLOR CODING?

Color coding your active file folders, disks, labels, rotary file address cards, calendar, and planner will save a lot of time when you need to locate a specific type of account or activity quickly. A quick glance and scan of these materials will give you an accurate view of your workload, deadlines, meetings, financial records, or whatever else is important in your work. You can also use a color-coded system to find related items within categories quickly, which makes the cross-referencing of paper files easier and more precise.

If the use of color coding to organize office information and services is so ideal, why doesn't everyone use this approach? The answer is simple. The procedure requires work and planning. To be effective, the system has to be used across the board. Every item of information must be correctly identified to make the system work, or the same confusion that usually results from incorrectly setting up alphabetical or numerical file systems will occur. But don't let this deter you from using color coding. Although you may have to do a little more work when you begin the system, the results are worth that effort because you save a significant amount of time in using the system.

Before beginning to purge your files and to go through the steps in organizing your files (Chapter 10), decide how many *broad* categories you will need and which colors you will use. This is not the time to view your options too narrowly. Although you can create as many specific categories as you wish, your system will be too complicated if every specific file category is assigned a separate color. You may also find that too few distinct colors exist to accommodate such numerous files.

Consider the problems that ensue when too many colors are used to identify too many categories.

Jake, a file clerk in a bookstore, thought that the concept of color coding was perfect for the bookstore files, because the nature of the business naturally lends itself to categories and divisions according to book type and topic. After an enthusiastic start, an early disaster made Jake feel like giving up, but he was successful after taking a more conservative approach to selecting broad categories and decreasing the number of his color choices.

Situation 9

Jake was assigned the task of reorganizing the active files and purging no longer needed information from the records of the bookstore for which he worked as a file clerk. His office manager was overwhelmed by new responsibilities and authorized him to restructure the system completely, so Jake decided to institute color coding to make locating documents easier. In an attempt to be systematic in his approach, Jake listed the following categories among a larger number that he hoped to create: *Animals, Arts, Autobiography, Biography, Business Expenses, Calen-*

dars, Cars, Children's Books—Fiction, Children's Books—Nonfiction, Cookbooks, Crafts, Crime, Inventory, Mysteries, New Age, Politics, Publishers, Reference, Romance, Short Stories, Sports, Tax Records, Travel.

Although not complete, the list became unwieldy and Jake realized that he could not possibly find enough different colors to accommodate the many items on his list. Furthermore, using so many different colors would only be confusing and would offer no improvement over simply labeling and alphabetizing the folders.

Jake's Solution

Once he recognized the unwieldy nature of his list, Jake decided to group his topics under four logical headings and to assign a color to each. For the structure of the bookstore accounts, the following broad categories proved to be useful:

- **Inventory** (blue)—Separate file folders are created to represent each type of book and item that the store sells.
- **Financial** (green)—Separate file folders are created to hold bank records, tax records, income, and business expenses.
- **Reference** (black)—Separate file folders are created to contain information regarding industry changes that affect the legal and publishing aspects, as well as industry trends.
- **Legal** (red)—Separate file folders are created to contain individual actions, judgments, liens, contracts, and other legal documents.

Jake used the colored labels to consistently identify all subcategories of the broader category as well as all individual file folders with the same identifying color. By doing so, he really eliminated a lot of the work that normally makes filing such a difficult and time-consuming job, because he can now easily sort out the broad categories of topics that may be piled in a stack of folders waiting in the "in" box to be filed. All he has to do is sort by color. After doing so, organizing the stack of folders within each color group is a much more manageable task.

Would this system work in your office? Of course it would, but careful step-by-step preparation must occur, and color coding should extend to other areas of organization in the office. Once you have decided on a color-coding system for your filing and created the necessary categories, you can extend the use of color coding to include related records. This approach to organization takes significant start-up time, but the results will save you a great deal of time as you work.

HOW CAN YOU EXTEND THE USE OF COLOR CODING?

How might this method of organization work in your office? Let's see how you might use the system of color coding that has already been applied to the filing system to increase efficiency in other areas. Reconsider Jake's color choices for the "Financial" and "Legal" categories, and apply these examples to color coding other areas.

Color Coding Computer Files

Let's see how color coding can be applied to computer files. Before doing anything further, Jake worked with the bookstore owner to review information already stored on the bookstore computer. Together, they purged no longer needed files and gave new names to active files to make them consistent in name with the paper files that Jake had already reorganized and color coded. In backing up the files on disks, Jake used green disks to back up "Financial" files and red disks for the "Legal" files. When Jake needs to access specific information that might be supplemented by invoices or contracts already filed in paper files, he can quickly locate what he needs by sorting through disks of the appropriate color category.

Color Coding Other Office Resources

You can further increase your efficiency at work by color coding the rotary file cards that contain addresses and telephone numbers and entries on calendars and planners. By using the same color choices, you can make them correspond to already color-coded files. To begin this effort, review the names of individuals and businesses that are contained on the cards in your rotary card file. Many addresses may have changed, some companies may no longer be in business, and other companies may no longer be doing business with the company that employs you.

Review all the names, addresses, and telephone numbers, and remove all the cards that list businesses that no longer exist or which you no longer deal with. Then obtain labels in the colors that you have already decided to use and apply them to cards to identify people and businesses that relate to one of the main categories. Thus, in the example given earlier in this chapter, Jake would apply green labels to those people and businesses that related to the "Financial" category, such as accountants, bank officers, bank departments, and others.

When you return the cards to the rotary card file, you can file them as before, because neither the files nor the address cards need to be grouped by color when they are filed. You can use any alphabetical or numerical system—and the categories will remain easily identifiable because of the colored labels. The key to success in color coding is to make each color relate to a distinct general category.

At the same time, don't become upset if you find that some files seem to belong in two different color categories. For example, the attorney retained by the bookstore owner to review tax law and to advise the bookstore owner regarding legal changes is coded with both green and red. When Jake has to locate the attorney's telephone number, he can immediately access the number without having to flip through the alphabetical listing because the dual color coding provides instant recognition.

Use the same color coding in writing information in your paper calendar or planner. Buy pens with the color ink that corresponds to the colors you assigned to each general category, and use the appropriate color ink to write meeting times and other information about appointments. If you have chosen to use the color green to indicate "Financial" information, you will use green ink to write in the times of meetings with the accountant, the Internal Revenue Service, or anyone else with a financial link. If you have chosen red to represent "Legal" concerns, then both your appointment for the building inspection by the town fire marshall and the meeting with your attorney will appear in red ink.

How many colors does your office need to cover all the categories of its operation? That is a question that you will have to answer yourself, because the organizational needs of each company are different. Try to keep the number of colors as low as possible, because too many colors will only create more confusion. And that confusion is what you are trying to avoid. You should aim to keep the number at four, and some companies have even found that two categories —Income and Expense—are enough.

NEXT STEP

Information in this chapter has revealed ways you can use color coding to extend your organizational techniques to all areas of office operation. In the next chapter, you will identify various means of creating room for everything that you need to become completely organized at work.

CHAPTER 12

CREATING A PLACE FOR EVERYTHING

Everything seems to be organized. Your desk contains neatly arranged "in" and "out" boxes, the telephone and electric pencil sharpener are out of the way but available, and the computer is conveniently placed. The desk area contains all necessary equipment, placed within arm's reach and out of the way of traffic. The files have been purged, relabeled, and color coded. This may be the most organized that you have ever been at work.

You probably feel very satisfied with your progress by this point—and you should be—but you are not ready to stop now. Not yet. The time has come to move away from the desk and the file cabinet—and to turn your attention to organizing the rest of your work area.

WHAT IS LEFT TO ORGANIZE?

Look around your desk and at the area near where you sit. Can you change anything else in the office to bring you closer to your goal of getting organized at work?

- Is the bulletin board covered with outdated notes, plans, cards, and memos?
- Are the bookshelves sagging under the weight of never-touched books, manuals, boxes, and other items?
- Is the vertical file holder stuffed with files that should be purged?

If the answer to any of these questions is "yes," then you still have work to do. Although the items left to organize are different, you will apply many of the same skills that you have already used in cleaning and organizing your desk area and filing systems.

As you sort and purge items, try to find additional ways of using the bulletin board, bookshelves, and vertical file holder. Are there creative uses to this space that you have overlooked?

Bulletin Boards

Is your bulletin board so covered with papers held by pushpins that you can barely see a part of the frame? Most of us are guilty of the same bulletin board abuse. We pin a note and leave it on the board "for now," but "now" often becomes weeks or months. By the time that we take the note down and plan to deal with it, we have usually forgotten its importance.

Your bulletin board can be a valuable aid at work, but first you have to organize it. Begin this task by removing every business card, every scrap of paper, every office memo, and every envelope from the bulletin board. Pile them on your desktop—your *newly organized* desktop—and use the same methodical system to sort these items that you used when you cleaned the desktop and sorted the stacks of papers and other clutter. This time, however, create two piles of material: those to save and those to discard. Throw away any duplicate business cards, outdated memos, and papers containing notes that no longer have any meaning for you or which contain times or dates of events long past.

Have you also pinned on the board postcards from friends or personal photographs? Make the same decisions about them—either throw them out or take them home. Keep it strictly business.

Now tackle the pile of items that you have saved, and match the information against your rotary card file, planner, calendar, or files. An important part of getting organized at work means not needlessly duplicating information. Throw away the business cards of people who are already in the rotary card file, and enter the names and other vital information for those who are not. If the information is worth saving, then it should be placed in a permanent file where you can readily access it. Proofread each new entry to make certain that you have accurately entered the information, then throw away the card.

Read each scrap of paper and decide if the information should be entered into a file folder, or into the rotary card file, calendar, or planner.

Use the following questions to guide you in your decision:

- Does the paper contain information about a meeting?
- Does it contain a personal telephone number?
- Is it a reminder of something important?
- Is it a note about an account or client?

The nature of the information contained on the paper determines where you will store it. If you determine after taking a second look that the scrap of paper is worthless, discard it.

If, however, you have found through experience that the information in such notes often becomes extremely valuable and that you remember the purpose *after* discarding, create a "holding tank" to store such notes temporarily. Place these "mystery notes" in a small box or even into a clean plastic sandwich bag. Label the outside with the date, and put it aside for two weeks. After two weeks, review the notes and, if they still have no importance, discard them.

Once you have cleared the bulletin board, use the space as a temporary storage space for information. Treat the board in the same way that you treat the "in" box, and clean it daily, filing what is important and discarding what is not. Instead of loading the board with push pins to hold random scraps of paper for an indefinite amount of time, save this space for really important reminders.

Bookshelves

In most offices, the bookshelves are used to hold everything that can't be placed elsewhere. Boxes of papers, old reports, outdated or useless equipment and parts, and a range of other items usually compete for space with books, manuals, and software. If the condition of your office bookshelves is similar and the shelves are sagging under the weight of messy piles of papers and worthless clutter, now is the time to clear those shelves of everything.

Before doing anything else, take inventory and see how many types of material you have placed on the shelves: books, reports, boxes of supplies, manuals, software, and anything else. Remove *everything* from the shelves and stack the different items into piles, each one containing a specific type of item. Check with your supervisor regarding what to do with the parts and equipment, and place them where a manager or someone else with the appropriate decision-making power can determine their fate. Then turn your attention to the remaining clutter. Having all of this in front of you provides the opportunity for more easily assessing which items are outdated and no longer needed.

Sort through any papers that have been stacked on the shelves and follow the organizational procedures that you used in cleaning your desk. Many of the old reports and documents may belong in the archive files, and many others may simply be trash. Once you have separated them, put aside the papers that you will file later, then move to the next set of items and work on organizing them.

How you organize these items depends on what they are. Your company may own many software manuals and software disks, but the shelves may contain few books. Another company may use the bookshelves to house many books but they may own few pieces of software. And a third company might have still different items on their bookshelves.

Sort through everything and remove all outdated software and books. How can you decide which to keep? Review the software that your company is currently running.

- If your company used to run only software for DOS but all computers have now changed to a Windows operating system, then the DOS-based software and companion manuals are outdated.
- If the company has completely replaced older computers with new computers, perhaps moving from PCs to Macintosh computers, the software and manuals related to the older computers are outdated.
- However, if your company has simply *upgraded* its software from a lower functioning version to a higher functioning version, for example from Windows 95 to Windows 98, keep the software and the manuals related to both.

After sorting out the software and manuals, speak with your boss to learn what your company's policy is regarding the no-longer-useful software and manuals. Some companies donate outdated materials to area schools or charities and receive a tax deduction, whereas others simply give away or discard the items.

Having completed that work, the next step is to organize the remaining books, manuals, and software in a way that is most suitable to your needs. How you organize the material depends on how much room you have available and how frequently they are used. If you have enough shelves to separate the types of items, you might place the books on one shelf, software on another, and manuals on the remaining shelves. With this arrangement, you can increase the effectiveness of your approach by alphabetizing the materials within each group so that you don't have to search through an entire shelf to find what you need. Books, in particular, are easier to find when they are first grouped together according to subject then alphabetized. To better organize the computer-related materials, pair the manuals with the related software, as well as with those books that are directly related to the software. Keep the material together on the shelves, even if you must mix books, manuals, and software.

As you arrange items on the shelves, you may decide that you or your coworkers frequently consult several of the books or the manuals more than others. In that case, place these items on your desk for much easier access to them. After you finish organizing, create a master list of the reorganized bookshelves, taking care to number the shelves and identify the holdings of each shelf and the order of the items. If others in the office use the bookshelves, as well, make several copies of the list, post a copy near the bookshelves for easy reference, and distribute copies to your coworkers.

Vertical File Holders

You may have created additional storage by placing a vertical file holder on the desktop, but over time it has become cluttered. When you cleaned your desktop, you may have ignored the file because it stands as a separate unit. Even if the papers are in folders and do not touch the newly organized desktop, you still have to address this problem.

A vertical file is an extremely valuable tool for creating order, but it is useless when used merely as a dumping ground. Treat this file as a separate entity, and begin by cleaning everything out of the folders and discarding what is unnecessary. You should use the same method and means of judging papers that you used in organizing the desk area and filing system. Review the labels on each folder, and change any that are no longer effective. Create labels that reflect accurately the materials that you place in the file. You may find that the following divisions are useful: "To Do," "Follow Up," "Projects," "Correspondence," "Bills to File," and other items that might usually appear in the "in" or "pending" boxes. Some papers may no longer be needed, and others should be filed in your active or reference files, so make these decisions as well. As for the papers that remain, file them in the individual files of the vertical file holder, then address them as quickly as you can.

As you place the newly organized vertical file folder on your desk, make up your mind to control the clutter and to keep papers from piling up.

WHAT HAVE YOU FORGOTTEN?

Are there any other areas of the office left to organize before we move on to using technology? Yes, but these areas are either not always the responsibility of any one office worker or they are not available to all workers. The reason is that all offices are not structured in the same manner. This difference affects two areas: the storage cabinet or closet and the use of office or cubicle walls.

Storage Cabinets or Closets

The storage cabinet or closet is usually ignored by many of us when we clean or reorganize our offices. Too often, we think of the space as necessary but unimportant; this is a mistake because a storage closet or cabinet can be put to an extremely important use when space is short in other places.

If you share the storage closet with others in the office, you may be able to enlist their help. Begin your task of organizing the storage area by first removing everything and placing the items on the floor. Decide what must stay and what can be discarded, using the following questions to guide you in making your decisions:

- Is this item needed?
- How soon do I plan to use this item?
- Even if the items are new and in unopened packages, is there a valid reason to keep them?
- Does the storage closet provide enough space to house the item?

After removing all of the supplies and other items, clean the shelves of the empty closet or cabinet, then prioritize here as you did in organizing your desk. If the closet does not contain enough shelves, ask the maintenance department to install additional shelves along the side and the back of the closet to provide more room for storage. You should also install hooks, because you might be able to suspend some items, which will provide you with additional storage space.

Once the closet is clean and you have made all possible modifications, sort through the items that you removed earlier. Decide which supplies or other items are most important and used most frequently, and place them on shelves that are most accessible to you. Place those items that you use less frequently onto the higher, harder-to-reach shelves.

To avoid buying duplicate supplies or misplacing files or other items that you store in the closet, assign a specific purpose to each of the shelves. Label the shelves clearly so that you and others will not waste time moving boxes around as you search for items on the wrong shelves. Your labels might include "Supplies," "Literature," "Archived Files," "Magazines," or anything else that your company needs to store. You might not make much use of mailing materials, so one shelf can be devoted to them, including the "out" basket, stacks of letterhead and envelopes, packaging for shipping, and the postage machine or stamps.

Now that you have identified a specific place for everything in the storage closet, be obsessive about maintaining that order. You will able to find what you want more easily if you are strict about replacing everything after it is no longer needed.

Wall Space

Some of us are fortunate to have our own separate offices and others share space with coworkers in areas that are divided by cubicle walls. Most office workers, however, share space in large rooms that have no dividers between the desks. For workers in this last category, very little physical space is left to organize. If, however, you either have your own cubicle surrounded by three walls or you have your own office, then your walls also provide potential storage space.

You may already use your walls as large bulletin boards, pinning messages, memos, phone numbers, calendars, and other reminders to the cubicle walls. Some workers with offices have upright files permanently attached to a wall, and they temporarily place documents in these files and sort them at the end of each day.

Another good use of a wall is to arrange for it to hold a large calendar on which to record appointments, deadlines, and other time-dependent information. Using the techniques of color coding that you learned in Chapter 11, you can coordinate your desk calendar and planner with the wall calendar to identify important dates using the same color marker or ink. You may feel that having the desk calendar would be sufficient, but the wall calendar provides a quicker visual scan of your day, and the use of color makes identifying what you have to do even easier. You might also find that this is a benefit to you in another way, because your schedule is displayed where coworkers and others can see it.

The walls are also valuable for posting other information that you wish to share with coworkers, such as copies of the file master list, and the lists of material stored on the bookshelves and in the storage closet.

As valuable as such wall space may be, it also poses a hazard. Having so much space on which to post data might lead you to misuse the walls and turn them into a much larger version of the bulletin board. If so, then you must take the same precautions that you do to keep the bulletin board organized. Scrutinize daily what you have posted on your walls and frequently discard unnecessary items. Don't waste wall space.

NEXT STEP

In this chapter, additional areas in the office that would benefit from a new or redesigned system of organization were identified, and suggestions were provided to create a more effective work atmosphere. In the next section, you will learn ways to make technology take over some of your tasks as well as ways in which the computer can help you to get organized at work.

SECTION IV

GETTING ORGANIZED WITH TECHNOLOGY

The business world has entered a new era, an electronic era, due largely to the development of such innovative technology as the facsimile (fax) machine, the personal computer (PC), and electronic mail (e-mail). Business is conducted over telephone lines that transfer documents over thousands of miles in only a matter of seconds. You can now receive documents in New York City that a bidder in Djakarta, Indonesia, may have sent via fax only minutes earlier.

Technology has expedited the way we conduct business, but it has also imposed burdens. If we are to take full advantage of the benefits of these developments, we must stay in touch with and remain well educated regarding changes that occur continuously in the area of information technology. For most businesses today, the company that can deliver its product or service most quickly while offering the best value will be the winner. To even become a competitor, however, a company must be structured to win—and technology is the means to getting organized at work.

CHAPTER 13

EXPLOITING THE POTENTIAL OF FAX AND E-MAIL

This chapter covers what for most business people is familiar technology, because the fax machine and e-mail have become catchwords of the business world. Even businesses that do not have fax machines will occasionally use the technology because many copy shops, business products stores, mailing and packaging services, and other stores offer fax transmission and receipt services for a fee.

E-mail has also become a technology that is familiar to most employees, even if a company does not provide them with e-mail accounts or have its own server. The popularity of personal home e-mail accounts has made competent e-mail communicators of many of us, even if we do not use e-mail at work. We also know how valuable such communication would be in the office.

The telephone and regular mail, dubbed "snail mail" by many, continue to be the main means of communication in business, but this is slowly changing. For many businesses, first class mail is even too slow, and the willingness of companies to pay premium prices for faster service has led to success for express mail services, which guarantee next-day delivery of mail. For a growing number of companies, even next-day delivery is not enough, because they want the nearly instantaneous transmission and response that they can obtain through fax and e-mail transmission.

Even if your company has not yet joined the push to make greater use of these technologies, you may find that making more use of them yourself will make you better organized at work.

By the end of this chapter, you will be able to do the following:

- Identify the appropriate time to use fax or e-mail.
- Learn to save time by sending information via fax.
- Learn to save time by sending information via e-mail.
- Learn how fax and e-mail can increase your organizational skills at work.

WHEN ARE FAX AND E-MAIL COMMUNICATION INAPPROPRIATE?

Sending information via fax or e-mail is a true time saver because you can send at any time—day or night—and you don't have to be present when people respond. Unlike telephone calls, even voice mail, both fax and e-mail provide you with hard copy to read, study, and keep, and you can respond at your convenience. The technology helps you organize your communications on your own schedule, because you avoid the lost time involved in waiting for the mail—even express mail—to arrive, and your schedule is not disrupted by having to wait for a telephone call.

The possibilities for how much time these technologies can save you and how much they can help you organize your workday seem endless. Still, extensive as the advantages may seem, their use is *not* appropriate as means of communication in all instances.

Unless speed is of the essence, do not send an important document via either means if the appearance of the original is vital to the recipient's appreciation of its value. Although plain-paper fax machines have eliminated the flimsy thermal paper of earlier models, many offices that do not send fax transmissions regularly still use them, and even photocopying the thermal page for durability does nothing to upgrade the appearance. Even the plain-paper fax versions are, at best, only copies. So, if the appearance of an original is important, use an express mail next-day service, and show the document to its best advantage.

Sending a document via e-mail is also not desirable if the appearance of the original is vital because distortion in the appearance does occur even when documents are scanned into or sent directly from a computer. The reason for this distortion is that the e-mail servers—yours and the recipient's—must translate the documents into readable format before they can send and receive. The cliché that is often applied to verbal misunderstandings is appropriate here, as well: "Something is lost in the translation." The information will transfer, but the carefully created appearance and format of the text may not.

You will find that even more of the aesthetic appearance is lost in transit if you send a long report as an attachment to the e-mail message. Such attachments are meant for you to download into a computer directory or onto a disk, then use your word processing program to open the file so that you can print it. If appearance is important, this is the worst possible way to send a document because it may have to go through three conversions. Two such conversions are mentioned above and the third conversion occurs when your word processor reads the file and translates it into the appropriate language for editing. Not much chance exists that the three conversions will maintain the original appearance of the document.

Aside from concerns regarding appearance, business etiquette requires that formal correspondence should be sent via regular mail, because these letters are meant to be kept, and their original condition and the original signature on the letter are important. You may argue that you can take a letter sent via fax, photocopy it if your receiving machine uses thermal paper, and file it, or simply file a letter received by a plain-paper fax, but the absence of the original signature and even the original appearance makes this choice undesirable. You will encounter the same problems if you choose to send formal correspondence via e-mail, even if you scan it into the computer. In using e-mail, you also face the potential problem of distortion.

You should also refrain from sending a letter via fax or e-mail if your boss has instructed you to obtain a signed return receipt from the recipient. Neither the message report that alerts you that the recipient has read your e-mail message nor the fax acknowledgment that prints at your end after you send the document is legal proof that a person has received your document. The law still requires an actual signature for such verification.

Using fax or e-mail to send documents is inappropriate in another instance: when privacy is a concern. Do not expect privacy in your transmission of material by either technology, because you will not find it. Therefore, do not send letters or documents that contain sensitive company financial information or confidential employee information. Everyone in the receiving office will have potential access to the fax transmission as it comes out of the machine and the person in charge of distributing messages stacks it with other letters. Even if only one or two unauthorized people read such information, ethical issues might arise. You cannot determine who will read your fax transmissions. You do not know who might be working at the receiving company and how other unauthorized individuals will use your information.

Do not make the mistake of believing that your e-mail transmissions are fully private at either end, because they are not. It is true that not just anyone can read your message, as might be the case with fax messages, but even deleted mail remains somewhere in server caches where people in the know can access them. Long after you may have forgotten messages that you sent and received, they can be found somewhere in the server files for an indefinite period of time, even after *you* no longer can access them—and the same is true of the receiver's server.

One more reason you should be concerned about sending sensitive or important documents via e-mail is the possibility of human error in addressing your message. The difference of one letter or number in an e-mail address can misdirect your communication and result in your sending sensitive files and data to the wrong person or company. Therefore, when privacy is of paramount importance, the use of fax or e-mail to deliver the information is inappropriate.

Now, with the negative aspects of these two technologies out of the way, let's move on to examining the many ways they can help you become better organized at work.

WHAT CAN FAX MACHINES DO FOR YOU?

The fax machine can save you a lot of time, because you can complete work on letters or documents late in the day yet deliver them via fax transmission before the business day ends. Knowing that you have such flexibility permits you to schedule other, more pressing work that might have to reach the package shipping counter or the post office before it closes. Your deadlines to complete work actually become more generous when you are able to send a document via fax. Other features, such as polling and broadcast, can increase your time flexibility and allow you to plan in advance long tasks that might take up the better part of a day.

An additional benefit is that, unlike other such useful tools, fax transmission is not a technologically complex operation, and you do not need training to learn to send documents in this way. All that you need is a standard telephone line, an electric outlet, and a fax machine, and you can send images of photographs, signatures, graphic designs, legal documents, and text. The value of this convenience is greater if your company uses employer photo identification cards or needs to ascertain that certain employees possess other valid identification, such as photo drivers' licenses.

Consider the following situation.

Situation 10

Tim is the assistant dispatcher in a trucking company that has sites throughout the northeastern United States. During key holidays, the company usually ships more packages out of certain sites than others, so personnel from less busy sites are temporarily reassigned and given generous bonuses to compensate them for the disruption in their lives. When these reassignments occur, management at the new sites requests copies of employee photo identification badges as well as copies of drivers' licenses to retain in their files. Tim has usually had ample time to make photocopies and send them out via certified mail, but recent management changes interfered with the most current set of reassignments, and the process was delayed.

After receiving a last-minute directive to proceed, the head manager at Tim's site panicked on the Friday morning before the reassignments were to occur. He knew that the company offices would not be open on Saturday or Sunday to receive copies via a next-day mail service. The manager also knew that even the best of the express mail services would not have the copies in the site managers' hands by 6:30 a.m. Monday morning when the first trucks were supposed to roll out.

As his superior panicked, Tim calmly pulled the copies of each driver's identification badge and license from the file that had been set aside as they awaited management approval. From his computer, he printed out an already created fax cover sheet template (you will learn how to create templates in Chapter 14) on which he listed the names and numbers of all eight sites with a note that only those copies relevant to the given site were being sent. He sorted the copies into eight piles, according to where the drivers were to report. With the company fax directory in front of him, Tim dialed eight fax numbers and sent a different pile of copies through for each. Within 20 minutes, all of the material had been transferred—and all before time for the midmorning break.

Later that day as Tim's supervisor called managers at the other sites and took credit for the speedy solution, Tim enjoyed an afternoon relaxing with his feet on the desk and a cup of coffee at his side—compliments of his grateful supervisor.

Could a similar situation occur in your company? Very likely. Tim could have panicked along with his supervisor, but he did not because he had already learned what the fax machine could do to make his work easier. In previous situations, when the company had needed shipping documents sent quickly, he had used the fax machine and then followed up by mail with copies that could be placed into permanent files.

Tim would have had an even quicker solution if the same documents were going to many sites, because he would have just used the broadcast feature of the fax machine. Using this feature, he could have programmed the list of fax numbers for sites that should receive the information, then allowed the machine to take over and send identical copies to all the sites.

Another feature of fax technology that will help you get organized at work is polling, which is used to make another machine send a document to your machine. Thus, you use your receiving machine to activate the transmission. Of course, you cannot do this with any fax machine that you choose for the obvious security reasons. The fax number and the system number of your machine must be entered in the secured machine to indicate that your machine has permission to poll it. As another option, you can also save time by permitting other fax machines to poll your office fax machine. To do so, you simply set the reception mode switch on your machine to "auto" and load your documents as you normally do. The polling machine calls your machine in the usual fashion and activates polling. Using this feature, you don't have to be present at the machine to send, and busy signals from either end are not impediments to the process, because the machines can redial automatically until a successful transfer occurs.

The polling feature is valuable to help you and your company save time and remain organized, but you have to obtain permission from both your manager and from the other company for the function to activate.

HOW CAN YOU GET THE MOST FROM E-MAIL?

Using electronic mail requires that you have access to a computer with a modem, telephone line, communications software, and an electronic mail service. Your office computers probably came packaged with everything that you need to begin using e-mail, but your office will have to assign you an e-mail address and connect you with a service.

To use e-mail effectively to get better organized at work, you will have to check your account at least once daily. You should also have access to and responsibility for the company's general e-mail account which receives client messages, if you are going to expedite work in the office. If you only work with the e-mail that arrives in your account, you will be dealing with a more limited aspect of company business, if you are dealing with any of the business at all.

The benefits of e-mail are many. E-mail allows you to respond instantly to messages, by simply typing in your response and clicking the "reply" button. You don't have to use letterhead or prepare an envelope as you must when you send snail mail. You also do not have to deal with the frustrations of making a telephone call and hoping that your party is present. Using E-mail also helps you avoid the dreaded "telephone tag" game, because you can respond to messages without having to make direct contact with the sender.

E-mail is more economical than fax transmission, because you can send messages locally or thousands of miles away for the same cost of a local call. This is one advantage over the fax machine, which accrues long distance call charges for long documents sent to distant sites.

E-mail is also convenient because you can send a message at any time of day or night, and you can read your respondent's reply with the same freedom. The message waits until you and your recipient are free to access it. You are not limited to simply brief messages, but you can attach long files when you want to transfer a report or even a book manuscript. If your office computer has a scanner, you can even scan pictures, graphics, and text into your computer and then send this information as an attachment, although the earlier warning regarding distortions in transmission should be taken seriously. In addition, you can program your software to save all of your incoming and outgoing messages in an electronic file cabinet, thus to maintain a complete record of your electronic correspondence. If you do so, be careful of what you send, because it might come back to haunt you.

Which technology should you choose? The decision really depends on your resources and your needs. Fax transmission and e-mail offer different features that can help you greatly in scheduling and organizing your responsibilities at work because they offer flexibility in when you send information, leaving you free to do other work. Which you choose depends on the nature of your company's business and the amount of responsibility that you have in the company.

NEXT STEP

We have examined in this chapter the ways fax and e-mail technologies can help you get organized at work. In the following chapter, you will learn how to organize your computer files and to create subdirectories and templates that will make you more efficient on the job.

CHAPTER 14

ORGANIZING YOUR COMPUTER FILES

Businesses of all types and sizes today use computers to store client data, manage transactions, process correspondence, and communicate. Even small one- or two-person offices find that a computer is essential to daily operations.

You may have formed some type of bond with a computer at work or at home and have a healthy respect for how computers can assist you in various tasks. Yet, like most of us, you may refrain from letting the computer complete all of your office operations. Some people are especially reluctant to transfer manually completed tasks to the computer.

Are you one of these people? Are you afraid of putting too much information on your computer, because you dread losing the work should the computer crash? Or, are you just not certain of how much the computer can do to make your life at work easier?

Either way, you are ignoring a business principle that most company managers have realized—increased efficiency means increased profits, and the computer can increase the efficiency of employees.

How, you may ask, will organizing your computer files help the company that you work for post increased profits? Through example, this chapter will answer that question, and it will provide you with the information and the tools necessary for organizing your computer files and the computer skills necessary for leading you into the 21st century.

This chapter assumes that you have a basic understanding of computer terms and a working knowledge of at least one of the many word processing programs available today.

By the end of this chapter, you will be able to do the following:

- create electronic subdirectories,
- back up your hard drive via two methods, and
- create templates and other generic files.

HOW CAN YOU CREATE ELECTRONIC SUBDIRECTORIES?

The key to getting organized is thinking in an organized way. Your computer files are a lot like your paper files, and the way to create order is the same for both. If you think of the computer directories as file cabinets and the subdirectories as the broad categories in a file drawer that contain groups of related folders, you will have an easier time organizing your computer files.

The computer subdirectories are your major topic divisions. For example, in setting up a computer filing system, a real estate company might divide its directories into the subdirectories of "Rental Properties," "Lease Properties," and "Sale Properties." Each category or subdirectory might be divided into subfolders for "Commercial" and "Residential," and each of these subfolders might further be divided into sub-subfolders containing information about individual properties. The computer files might be organized in this manner:

Folder: "Lease Properties"
    Subfolder: "Residential"
        File: "50 Main Street"

The computer will not do the thinking for you—it will only follow your directions—so be careful to develop the right names for your folders and files. You have to think carefully about the use of key terms and comprehensive labels for your paper files, and you have to do the same with computer documents. The names that you give your files have to make sense and relate to the work that you are filing and saving, or else you will run into serious confusion when you attempt to retrieve the file. If the name of a file is not descriptive enough to identify its content, you might spend hours scrolling through file names and opening files to view their contents—hardly an efficient method of organization!

Let's take the example of Bernie, a recently hired account agent at a property management firm.

Situation 11

Bernie has just completed a lucrative deal negotiating a lease and working out the details with the client. He has just created a new copy of the lease on his word processing program and saved it to his hard drive. When saving the file, Bernie named the document **Lease #2**, then pressed the "Save" button and sent the document into the memory banks of his computer. A year later, Bernie receives a phone call from the tenant, who wants to renovate part of the building. Business has been good for Bernie during that year and he has negotiated and renegotiated numerous leases during that time. He tells the client that he will first have to review the lease before giving any written or oral approval. Then Bernie turns on his word processing program and begins to search for the lease through various titles and directories. After almost an hour, he finds the directory where the leases are saved, only now he can't remember what he named the lease, so Bernie must open each document until he finds the correct one.

Does this scenario sound familiar to you?

If the answer to the above question is a resounding "yes," don't worry, you are not alone. However, enduring this painstaking process costs you time, and it costs your company money. So, what can you do to eliminate this problem?

Bernie's Solution

Let's look at an alternate scenario, with the same players in the same situation. After Bernie successfully negotiates the deal and finishes creating his lease, he clicks on the "Save As" button. He then moves his mouse over a series of buttons until he finds the one marked "Create New Folder." He clicks on that button and follows the directions to give the folder the new title of "1997 Leases." Bernie then gives the file containing the lease the title of "Lease for 50 Main St." Bernie clicks on the "Save" button, and he is done.

A year later, when Bernie receives the same phone call as before, he has no problem locating the specific lease. This time, he simply tells the client, "Hold one second while I get your lease." Bernie then opens his word processing program, goes to the folder labeled "1997 Leases," finds the document labeled "Lease for 50 Main St.," and double clicks on that icon. Within seconds, the lease appears on Bernie's computer screen.

The key concept to remember in organizing your computer files is to think of the computer as a filing cabinet. "Windows 95" makes it very easy to think in such a way. "Explorer" is your filing cabinet, and it holds all the documents that you have created and saved. However, just as when filing paper you do not place documents randomly in any part of the filing cabinet (See Chapter 10), you should not place Windows documents in just any order. In the same way that you create and label folders in which to store paper documents, do the same in the electronic world. You will find that storing documents electronically will become easy, if you follow a few simple guidelines:

- Remember that the computer can act as a gigantic filing cabinet, using subdirectories that act like filing folders.
- Never just save material loosely; instead, save it into a specific folder.
- Make your life easier by specifically labeling all of your documents and your folders.
- Use dates in your labels whenever possible.
- Don't forget that time is money and the less time you spend searching for documents, the more time you can spend on other, revenue-producing ventures.

WHY BACK UP THE HARD DRIVE?

Backing up the hard drive is very similar to making a business deal: You have to make all the necessary preparations, take all the necessary precautions, and give attention to all of the details.

Consider two possible approaches to the same scenario. You are having a power lunch with a prospective client, but you were late for work and pulled your clothes together hurriedly. You rushed out of the office after your midmorning break, and your breath still reeks of coffee because you forgot your breath mints at home. Although both you and the client are supposed to focus on the financial aspects of the potential deal, the chances are good that your omissions are going to hurt your prospects of landing the client.

Now, let's create a second scenario. You prepared carefully for the appointment, dressed carefully, and have made certain that your breath smells like peppermint. Granted, this attention to personal detail won't land you the deal, but your preparation and personal comfort will convey confidence, and you will not distract the client with negative aspects of your grooming. These factors will increase your chances of landing the deal far more than if you had not taken these measures.

What does this have to do with backing up your hard drive? Just as the attention to personal detail will not guarantee a deal but will increase your advantage, backing up the hard drive will not increase revenue or decrease immediate expenses, but it is a must for the businessperson.

Let's return to Bernie, who has now developed a well-organized computer filing system, complete with properly labeled folders, subfolders, and files.

Situation 12

One day, while Bernie is busily working at creating a lease, his computer screen goes blank. He panics and restarts his computer, but the computer restarts with nothing on it. As Bernie sits there, sweat forms on his brow and the horror of the situation hits him—his hard drive has CRASHED!

Bernie has lost everything—all his leases, all his documents. *Everything* is gone. His first thought is, "My boss is going to kill me!"

If he were not afraid of alerting his boss to the disaster, he could contact a computer expert who *might* be able to restore the data on the hard drive. Even here, however, success is not guaranteed. Instead, Bernie tinkers with the computer, reinstalls the recovery disk, and finds that he has lost a substantial amount but not all of the files. To recover the rest, he spends the next few weeks secretly calling tenants to ask that they send copies of leases or any other duplicates of correspondence.

Bernie's work suffers, as he tries secretly to input all of the lost data and keep up with his usual work load. He also suffers because he is not sure that he can trust the tenants to send all of the paperwork that he needs nor that they will not tamper with it. His bosses take notice of his decreased efficiency and stressed behavior, and they are not pleased.

Could Bernie have avoided this disaster? Yes, and very easily by simply preparing in advance for such an event.

Bernie's Solution

Faced with the possibility of a hard drive crash, a more knowledgeable Bernie has prepared for the disaster well in advance and knows what to do. As before, his computer crashes, but this time it is not a career-ending experience. He simply opens his desk drawer and removes some computer disks from a case. These disks contain all his documents, leases, and other business correspondence. While reloading these documents onto the computer does, indeed, take some time, Bernie sighs in relief because he is prepared for this situation. He has copies of his original documents and does not have to contact tenants nor incur the wrath of his bosses. He may have to work a little harder and faster to make up for the time spent reloading the files, but the relief that he feels in having all the files easily makes up for that.

While Bernie's story may seem overly dramatic, it is not unique. All too often, we rely on the computer always to contain what we need and to respond as we command. Because the computer does not give warning of potential disaster, we are rarely prepared for it to crash.

Ask yourself this question. Would you leave valuable items at a repair facility or hand over a large amount of cash without receiving a receipt? Of course not, and you should never save a file to a hard drive without first backing it up.

You have two options for saving your work. The first way of backing up your drive is to save it to a floppy disk. This method involves saving folders and documents to multiple disks. This process is effective, but it can become tedious and costly. It is also quite primitive and takes up a lot of disk space, which will increase clutter around the office.

The second, and more high-tech, option for backing up the hard drive is to use a ZIP disk, which allows the user to save large quantities of information onto a special, high-capacity disk. The initial cost for the ZIP drive may be higher than for the disks, but you will save more money in the long run. First, you will not have to purchase the many floppy disks that would be needed to save an equal amount of data. Second, this process saves on user time, because the annoying task of inserting and removing multiple disks is not needed.

Whichever method you select, the following guidelines for backing up data apply:

- Remember the lessons in organization that you read earlier in this book? They also apply to saving your work. Create folders, and properly label all material.
- Make sure that your back-up disks are stored away from heat, telephone lines, and magnets, which could cause the loss of data.
- Always place labels on the disks and include correct file names and a brief synopsis of the contents.

HOW CAN YOU SAVE TIME WITH TEMPLATES?

Most of us are in a rush for most of our workday, and anything that will save time is welcome. To understand the importance that templates can have in helping you to get organized at work, consider a situation in which you are in a rush. You have 10 minutes to get to the Federal Express office, and it usually takes exactly that time to drive there. Suddenly, someone tells you of a quicker route, a route that will place you at your destination in five minutes.

Which route would you choose? The answer, of course, is the route that gets you there in five minutes.

An office template is a lot like taking the shorter route. It allows the user to produce unique-looking documents from a generic file. So, instead of creating a new fax cover sheet, letter of correspondence, report cover, or another standard document, all you have to do is open the correct file, fill in some unique information (such as the person's name, the date, etc.), and the document is ready to print. Using templates eliminates a lot of the time and monotonous "busy" work that seems to occupy so much of our working days.

You can use two methods working with templates. To see how effective templates can be, consider their use by Holly, an assistant in the Human Resources Department.

Situation 13

Holly is an administrative assistant in the HR department at a local hotel. She is in charge of answering phones, but she usually spends the bulk of her days typing acceptance and rejection letters to people who have interviewed for jobs at the hotel. Each day, Holly spends countless hours typing individual letters that tell people that either they are either accepted or rejected for employment. At the end of the day, Holly looks at the stack of paperwork on her desk and wonders where all the time in the day has gone and how she is ever going to get the rest of her work finished. As Holly looks back on her day and tries to find a way to gain extra time, she remembers the idea of the office template.

Holly writes her next letter accepting a new employee to the hotel. This time, however, instead of printing the letter and not saving it, she clicks on the "Save" button. A day goes by and Holly must write another acceptance letter, and this time she does not have to start from scratch. This time, Holly opens the letter she saved the other day, changes the date, the name, the address, and the position of the new employee, clicks the print button, and is free to return to her stacks of paperwork. Holly has just created a primitive template.

While the term "template" may initially sound like some computer jargon, it is actually just an old concept that has been given a high-tech feel. The above story constitutes the first way to create a template, and it is very effective, but you should stop with this method. Most word processing programs have hundreds of different templates, some with graphics, for a variety of office functions. What this means is that you don't even have to create the first document and save it, because the computer has already done it for you. All you have to do is select the template that suits your organization best, click on the "okay" button, and fill in the specific information, such as name, date, etc. Predesigned templates offered by the computer include templates for the following:

- purchase orders,
- letters,
- faxes,
- resumes, and
- invoices.

The template is the most powerful tool that we have discussed in this chapter. Not only will it save you time, but it will also standardize your documents and increase your efficiency in the office. To make this tool most valuable, you should develop your own templates, in addition to using the ones provided by the word processing program. Consult the manual that accompanies the specific word processing software to learn how to create templates.

We have covered quite a bit of material in this chapter that will help you organize your computer files. As you master each of the areas covered, place a check on the line below:

____ I know how to organize my hard drive into an electronic filing cabinet complete with well-labeled files and folders.
____ I understand and I am able to use both methods of backing up my hard drive.
____ I understand what a template is and how it can help each day at the office.
____ I know how to create my own templates.

Once you can place a check in all of the above boxes, pat yourself on the back, because you have taken a major step toward making your life easier and increasing your productivity at work. Congratulations!

NEXT STEP

In the next chapter, you will learn how to use your computer to eliminate clutter around the office. Not only will you eliminate those annoying sticky notes, but you will also learn the electronic secrets to never misplacing another phone number or missing another meeting.

CHAPTER | 15

ELIMINATING CLUTTER WITH YOUR COMPUTER

Are you using the computer for more than just word processing? If not, then you are not enjoying some of the many other features that would make your life easier and help you to eliminate clutter in your work area. New software also allows the computer to take the place of other office equipment, including the fax machine, so you can also increase your desk space by learning to exploit all of the computer's capabilities.

Before we examine what additional advantages you can enjoy, respond to the following checklist to identify the areas in which your needs lie. Place a check next to each question if the answer is "Yes."

____ Do you often misplace phone numbers?
____ Do you sometimes forget to take messages for yourself and others?
____ Do meetings and other engagements slip your mind?
____ Do you find yourself staying after the day ends to clean your work area each day?
____ Do you often sort through stacks of paper just to find the one item you need?

If the answer to any of these questions is "yes," then this chapter will help you greatly. Using the computer to perform many office tasks—such as message taking, schedule planning, and recording telephone numbers—allows you to reduce the amount of clutter that accumulates throughout the day. Furthermore, using this electronic media will make you more efficient in the office and improve your work through such methods as standardization, professionalism, and increased computer knowledge.

By the end of this chapter, you should be able to do the following:

- Eliminate the need to use Post-it pads for taking messages.
- Understand the basic framework of organizing software.
- Decrease the current level of clutter at your workstation.
- Save yourself time and your company money.

CAN YOU ELIMINATE THOSE PESKY STICK-ON NOTES?

Have you ever remained at the office during lunch break when everyone else was out? You are the only one there, then the phone rings. While you're answering one line, the next line rings, and then the next, and so on and so on.

By the time the phones finally stop ringing, you have written out so many stick-on notes that your desk is piled with paper, your hair is a mess from running your fingers through it in frustration, and now *you* need a break. As the others are about to return to the office, you sort out the notes, and realize that you methodically took messages—but you forgot to identify who the message was for on a few of the notes. Now you will have to face the wrath of coworkers, as well as your boss, who had several messages.

Faced with such a hectic situation, you are bound to mix up some of the messages, aren't you? What choice do you have? The phones have to be answered, and you have no control over how many incoming calls will ring at once. You have to write down the messages for the people, right? Not necessarily!

In this day of computer-facilitated magic, you are able to take messages without ever lifting a pen—just use your computer. Imagine this: A phone call comes in and you answer the call. The call is for your supervisor who is at lunch, and the caller wants to leave a message. Faced with this situation, your usual solution would be to locate the sticky pad, write out the message, time of call, and return number; then take the message to your supervisor's office and hope that she finds it when she returns from lunch. Is that your only choice?

No, your computer has given you another option. Consider how much easier your task can be if, as soon as the call were to come through, you clicked on to a message-taking screen that had a simulated sticky "while you were out" note on it. All you have to do is choose the person's name to send it to, check the appropriate box for the message (i.e. "will call back", "urgent," etc.), and click the word "Send." This message will now go directly into your supervisor's e-mail account.

This ability to record electronic telephone messages will save you time, energy, and the worry that accompanies the possibility of losing a note that could cost the company millions, and you, your job. You won't have to look far to find this program, because variations already appear in Microsoft Office and Corel 7, as well as other popular office software. You probably have this program already bundled as a part of your current office software package, but you have not yet discovered it.

Using the message software saves you from accumulating a chaotic mountain of sticky notes, while it provides another advantage. If you use electronic mail to forward the telephone messages to recipients, you should save every message that you send and receive within a certain period. If you do so, then your electronic filing cabinet will have a record of all your messages—and you will have none of the clutter that would occur if you were to save six months of telephone messages on paper.

Let's suppose that a call came in two or three days ago, and you took the message, using the old method of writing it on a sticky pad. Your boss returned to the office and you gave him the message, so that should have been the end, right? This is usually true, but the exceptions to what is usual are the sources of our stress. Two days after the call, your boss decides to follow up on the message and asks you for the phone number of the caller. So, you either have to tell him that you have long since discarded the sticky note and did not record the telephone number (why would you?), or go rooting through the trash in the dumpster before the scheduled weekly pickup, neither of which pleases you very much.

Don't panic, because technology offers a better solution to this potential problem. When you send electronic mail, you can save every message that you send, even the computerized telephone messages. Now, instead of searching through the trash or the dumpster when your boss demands that you locate the telephone number, you can turn on your handy PC, open the file that lists all the e-mail you have sent, and call up the program. Instantaneously, the number appears on the screen and the day is saved. Now you need not deal with the hassle or embarrassment of searching for lost notes, because everything is at your fingertips.

If you have been paying attention, you are probably about to ask, "If my boss received the telephone message via e-mail, why doesn't *he* have a copy on his hard drive?" He might—if he also saves all e-mail transmissions—but don't count on it. Because he asked *you* to obtain the number, and because you are probably already familiar with his reliance on you, be prepared to supply this and all information that you forward.

CAN YOU PLAN BETTER—AND MORE SAFELY?

In today's business world where would any of us be without our Filofax, Day Runner, or other daily planner? Recall the earlier discussion of their importance in planning and scheduling your life as you examined ways of managing your tasks (Chapter 7). These planners are the bibles of our lives, into which we entrust telephone numbers, appointments, addresses, and other details of our personal and professional lives.

If you have ever doubted the importance of such daily planners or personal organizers, ask people who have lost a planner what the consequences were. You will be startled by the reaction. When reflecting on the loss, they sound like sad children whose greatly loved puppy has run away. The worst part is that losing a Filofax is much more costly than losing a pedigreed puppy. The unlucky soul has to not only buy another planner but recreate his or her life on paper. This entails obtaining and reorganizing phone numbers, apologizing for missed appointments, and making amends for the general chaos that the loss of this item has created for many more people than just the owner.

The information technology age does offer a remedy for this problem that is both cost effective and easy to manage. Many office manager programs such as Lotus Organizer or Microsoft Office contain programs that act as virtual planners, with features to rival any paper planner. They combine address book, calendar, and planner functions; some even offer year-at-a-glance features and telephone log features that record the date, time, and duration of calls.

Now, instead of flipping through a rotary card file, you can just view the client's phone number on a computer. To make matters easier, most of these programs also have a function that commands the computer to dial the person's number for you.

Perhaps a more valuable facet of these computerized organizers is their use as daily planners. Instead of penciling in each appointment and trying to fit the phrases on the allotted amount of space, you can simply type in the appointment using as much or as little detail as you feel is necessary. Some programs will even interact with your computer's internal clock to alert you of an upcoming appointment or meeting.

If your company site is made up of several buildings and you move frequently between different buildings, you may find that a handheld organizer is more useful than using your computer as a planner. The virtual pocket organizer has revolutionized and will continue to revolutionize the way we take and record telephone calls, plan for meetings, and maintain a chronology of office events. Handheld organizers, such as the Sharp Wizard or the Casio Executive feature a calendar, scheduler, telephone book, simple word processor, and other features, and some even include Lotus 1-2-3 spreadsheet capability.

Electronic personal organizers also interface with computers, so you can transfer from the portable planner into your desktop computer to maintain a permanent record. Such capabilities provide you with portability while they reduce the clutter that accumulates in an office from the use of sticky pads and other notes. Furthermore, the use of such software helps you to be more efficient, thereby making you look better in the eyes of your present and future employers.

WHY WOULD YOU NEED A FAX MODEM?

You have already identified ways you can save time and make full use of all features of your fax machine to become better organized (Chapter 13). Those suggestions remain useful if you work in an office that contains a fax machine and if you are expected to make frequent use of it. If, however, you have a choice and if your computer has the capability, then you can increase your efficiency at work and become even *better* organized by using your fax modem.

We have discussed the use of templates as a strong tool in saving you time and effort (Chapter 14); the fax modem makes this tool even more powerful. Consider how different your response to the following task would be if you have read only up to Chapter 14 of this book:

Your boss tells you that he needs you to fax some documents out to a business associate of his, but you first have to create those documents. What do you do? Using all that you have learned about templates, you would open up the template file, choose the correct template, input the proper information, then print the document. Next, you have to walk to the fax machine, wait for others to finish faxing their documents, and go through the whole faxing process. This can be annoying and time consuming, especially if you have a long wait to get to the fax machine.

Of course, after reading this section, you may never again have to wait to use the fax machine. Many office manager programs, such as Corel 7 and Microsoft Office, have a built-in function called a fax modem; Windows 95 also contains this feature. This function allows you to create a cover letter, using either templates saved in your files or your own creations. You are prompted to tell the computer which documents you wish to send, then input the proper fax number for the receiver and click "Send." Voila, your boss's documents will be received faster than if you had waited for the cover letter to print and then for the office fax machine to become free.

The use of such a tool makes your life a lot easier and diminishes the amount of mindless busywork that infiltrates your days at the office. You can also edit right up to the point of sending the document, something that is not an option if you spot an error as you wait for your turn in the faxing line.

IS A LAPTOP COMPUTER NECESSARY?

Laptop computers have found an audience that is entirely different from the original market, which was made up largely of people who used them as portable and temporary tools. Data created was meant to be transferred to the desktop unit, but a growing number of companies have issued laptop computers to employees because of space limitations and the need to use employees in a range of tasks that do not require continued use of the computer. Instead, the laptop computer has become a valuable tool in helping people to become better organized at work.

Thus, your boss might ask you to take the laptop with you when you go to the company warehouse to obtain transaction data, and to input the data immediately. A growing number of companies have begun to issue laptop computers to employees who have to travel between buildings or even between sites separated by several miles. Loaded with word processing, spreadsheet, planning, and communication software, these computers provide employees with the means of remaining productive, even if they are several miles from their desktop units.

If you work for a physician who maintains two offices, you might use the laptop computer to transfer patient appointments and other patient data to the computers at each site. In addition, you can carry other work to complete at whichever site you are working that day.

The laptop computer has caught up with the desktop units in regard to speed and range of available functions. The newest laptops rival their big brother and sister PCs in these areas, as well in regard to disk storage size, printer interface variety, communications capability, and other features.

By integrating a laptop computer into your office, you can gain two important advantages. First, you save on the space and clutter that the normal, larger desktop computer generates. The second, and probably more important, advantage of the two is mobility. Many people use mass transportation to commute to and from work. This leaves several idle hours per day that could be spent in a much more productive way, and many employers are also developing financial arrangements to encourage such after-hours productivity.

To examine how a laptop computer might help you to become better organized, consider the effect that it has had on Sally, an executive assistant for a clothing manufacturer.

Situation 14

Sally loves her job as the assistant to a clothing manufacturer, even though she spends more than three hours each day commuting into New York City from her home in New Jersey. She has often stayed late into the night at the office, just to finish correspondence or other work that had to be completed on the computer. Besides creating a large inconvenience in her personal life, the late hours and later commute home have made her vulnerable to danger walking through the nearly empty office building and on her way to the Port Authority Bus Terminal.

After the police warned employers in the building to be cautious because several attacks had occurred at night in recent weeks, Sally spoke with her boss and asked to modify her hours. Her boss needed to have the work completed and knew that if Sally did not accept the overtime, the company would have to hire another daytime employee to get the work done. That would mean having to put another employee on the payroll, with all of the additional bookkeeping and cost of health benefits, tax and Social Security deductions, and other benefits, as well as the time and cost of training a new person. When Sally's boss weighed these costs against the price of a new laptop computer loaded with software—about $2,000—the choice was easy.

Sally received a laptop computer from her employer, and now she can leave work at the same time as her coworkers. This freedom allows Sally to walk to the bus station with her friends, in broad daylight, surrounded by hundreds of other people commuting to their homes. Once within the safe confines of the bus, Sally turns on her laptop and begins doing the same work that she would have been doing at the office. Her laptop has saved her time, and possibly even her life.

The laptop computer can greatly help you to get organized at work, but not every employer may see the need for supplying them to employees. If, however, your situation is similar to that of Sally, or if you have to work at different sites, you might approach your boss with the suggestion for a laptop computer.

In this chapter, we have examined a range of ways that computers can eliminate clutter in your office and help you to become more organized. As you master each of the areas covered, place a check on the line below:

____ I have learned how to organize my computer files to eliminate the need for sticky notes.

____ I have identified ways that a virtual organizer can be useful to my office.

____ I know how to save time by using such tools as the fax modem, computerized rotary card file, and event planner.

____ I understand the importance of a laptop computer and the many ways it can enhance productivity in the office.

No matter how efficient or careful you are in taking messages or appointments, something will eventually be lost, and the ramifications can be disastrous. By learning how to use virtual planners and organizers, you can save yourself time and worry. The same can be said for **fax modems** and laptop computers. While many offices do not make such items available to its staff, do not be afraid to ask. Tell your employer that such items will save money in the long run, and they will increase the efficiency and efficacy of that office. You should experiment with and incorporate these methods into your daily work life, because they will save time, decrease stress and spending, and increase productivity.

NEXT STEP

In the next chapter, you will examine the diverse ways you can use spreadsheets to complete many tasks in the office.

CHAPTER 16

USING SPREADSHEETS TO GET ORGANIZED

Spreadsheets—just a mention of the word conjures up images of accountants and CPAs wearing green visors and tucked away in stuffy cubicles where they are creating complicated and unintelligible financial charts. Many people believe that developing spreadsheets requires hard-to-learn software and that the use of spreadsheets is only applicable when extensive and complex data must be analyzed.

They're wrong. This image is not at all correct. In this age of computer facilitation in most areas of business, the spreadsheet has become a powerful tool that is now used to manipulate all sorts of data. From baseball managers to schoolteachers—whatever your profession—all of us can save time and organize our tasks with the help of the spreadsheet. Every profession that compiles data, whether that data is financial or statistical, can use the spreadsheet to become better organized.

By the end of this chapter you should be able to do the following:

- Understand how spreadsheets can be useful to you.
- Learn to create a spreadsheet.
- Understand some of the more advanced functions of spreadsheets.
- Save time in your daily routine by using spreadsheets.

IS THERE A SPREADSHEET FOR YOU?

As we examine what spreadsheets actually are and the ways they are useful, keep several thoughts in mind. First, because this book is written for people engaged in a wide array of professions, and because the authors of this book do not know your exact job, the discussion of what spreadsheets can do for you is, at best, general.

That is the bad news; however, here is the good news: No matter what your profession or position in a company, you will still benefit greatly from learning how to use a spreadsheet. The spreadsheet is a powerful tool that will help you to achieve success and greater efficiency.

Are you still not convinced that using spreadsheets can make you better organized—even if your tasks do not normally require data analysis? Review the following list, and place a check next to every task that you have to complete at work, even occasionally.

_____ Keep track of monthly business expenses for myself.
_____ Tabulate monthly business expenses for employees.
_____ Maintain listings of client telephone numbers and addresses.
_____ Maintain listings of employee telephone numbers and addresses.
_____ Calculate daily, weekly, or monthly expenses for supplies.
_____ Maintain invoice records.
_____ Track budgetary and nonbudgetary expenditures.
_____ Maintain employee benefits records.
_____ Maintain inventory records.
_____ Maintain employee attendance records.

If you checked even one of the above tasks, you can use a spreadsheet to organize your work more quickly and more accurately.

By now you suspect strongly that spreadsheets can be useful to you, but do you know what a spreadsheet is and how it can help you? At its most basic, a spreadsheet is a listing of numerical and qualitative data that is organized in such a way as to promote efficient interpretation of its content. Got that? While this definition is solid, it may indeed be a little too technical. Let's make the definition more intelligible. A layperson's definition for a spreadsheet is any sheet or chart that lists and organizes data. In the presentation of such information, the spreadsheet usually separates entries into distinct columns and rows, so that the relationship among the entries can be viewed and understood at one time. The spreadsheet resembles the accountant's old-fashioned ledger. The difference is that the spreadsheet software provides greater power and allows you to perform a range of very complicated calculations. Not only can you prepare financial reports and analyses, but you can use current data to calculate budgetary needs and to analyze difficulties—real and imagined—all with the click of your mouse.

To demonstrate the power and usefulness of spreadsheets, we will revisit the office of Bernie, whom you met in Chapter 14.

Situation 15

You will recall that Bernie works in a property leasing office, and he is responsible for carrying out a number of clerical and administrative duties. On this particular day, Bernie has been told to compile a list of invoice expenditures, for which he must also calculate the sales tax and any late fees that the company has accrued. To accomplish this overwhelming task, Bernie must first use a ruler to create a chart that contains four columns and numerous horizontal rows. After doing so, he must write in each invoice number and the price of each. In the third step of the task, Bernie must use his calculator to compute the sales tax values for each invoice. Next, Bernie must calculate and record any penalties that the company has incurred for late payment. Only after completing these steps can Bernie then total each column to obtain a listing of invoice expenses for the week.

Don't these numerous steps seem like a huge waste of time? If you said "yes," you are correct. Using a spreadsheet would simplify the task and enable Bernie to cut his work in half.

Let's take a look at how this task would be completed if Bernie turned to technology. This time, as soon as Bernie gathers the invoices for the preceding week, he switches on the computer and accesses his spreadsheet software. He then enters a listing of each invoice and price. His next step is to calculate the sales tax. Now, however, instead of doing it himself with a calculator and having to compute nine products, Bernie can simply tell the computer to multiply the invoice price by a specific percentage, and the computer will calculate the sales tax for each invoice. Bernie must next calculate any late fees the company may have incurred. However, just as with the sales tax, the computer can calculate every value in a matter of seconds, thus saving Bernie the time spent in performing the nine calculations.

After completing all of the steps, Bernie clicks the mouse and commands the program to add all the prices on the sheet to give him the invoice totals for the week.

Below is an example of what Bernie's spreadsheet would look like after all of the steps described have been completed:

INVOICES FOR THE WEEK 4/12-4/19

Invoice #	Amount	Sales Tax	Late Fees	Total
33453	$23.56	$1.41	$0.50	$ 25.47
22346	$12,343.54	$740.61	$261.68	$13,345.83
11234	$6,593.85	$395.63	$139.79	$7,129.27
24356	$334.32	$20.06	$7.09	$361.47
34897	$11,345.98	$680.76	$240.53	$12,267.27
45765	$4,456.87	$267.41	$94.49	$4,818.77
45987	$11.76	$0.71	$0.25	$12.72
45789	$3,346.66	$200.80	$70.95	$3,618.41
45894	$321.12	$19.27	$6.81	$347.20
Totals	$38,777.66	$2,326.66	$822.09	$41,926.41

Your first observation is most likely that this chart looks a lot neater and more professional than if Bernie had done this by hand. The second great advantage that Bernie obtains from using a spreadsheet to record and total his invoices is the guaranteed accuracy of his results. Had he used a calculator, one misplaced finger could have thrown off all of his calculations. If Bernie even became aware of his errors in time, he would have to recheck each calculation just to find where he went wrong. The final, and greatest, advantage that Bernie gains is time.

Let's compare the two systems:

- System 1 requires that Bernie draw the lines on each chart. When Bernie uses System 2, the computer draws the lines automatically.
- System 1 requires that Bernie compute each value individually using a calculator. When Bernie uses System 2, he enters a simple multiplication formula into the program and the computer does the rest.

- System 1 requires that Bernie total each column individually and then find a total amount spent for the week. System 2 allows him to click one mouse button and have the computer calculate the total for him.

You should now have a better understanding of how spreadsheets can help you throughout the course of the workday. However, the usefulness of a spreadsheet is not limited to computing sales tax and totaling the prices of an inventory. Instead, spreadsheets can be used for a host of different functions. Below is a list of some areas of your life that spreadsheets may help you with:

- keeping track of monthly expenses,
- listing phone numbers and addresses,
- performing mathematical equations that require the same action but with different numbers (e.g., the sales tax column on Bernie's spreadsheet),
- organizing your personal expenses, and
- budgeting for yourself and your department.

WHAT SHOULD YOUR SPREADSHEET LOOK LIKE?

Now that you understand how powerful a tool a spreadsheet can be—and how valuable it is in helping you to become better organized—you are ready to proceed to the next step, creating the actual spreadsheet. However, before we can begin with the actual sheet, review the following key terms with which you should familiarize yourself before proceeding:

Columns—the sections of the spreadsheet moving from the top to the bottom

Rows—the sections of the spreadsheet moving from left to right

Tabs—the part of the spreadsheet, usually located at the bottom of the sheet, that gives the sheet its name.

Once you have learned these terms you should be ready to begin creating your spreadsheet. Because every spreadsheet has its own idiosyncrasies, no real lesson can be given here regarding what exactly to do in all possible situations. However, there are four basic rules that apply to whatever program you are using.

- First, remember always to aim for a professional appearance with your spreadsheet. To do this, the format command becomes your best friend.

This is the command that allows you to adjust the height and width of your columns and rows. The format command can also create borders around the cells, change text to different colors, and fill in whole rows with color, as was done on the top line of Bernie's spreadsheet. The color would, of course, only be effective if you use a color printer.

- The second rule of creating a spreadsheet is always to check the formulas that you entered. Once you have gained more proficiency in the mathematics of spreadsheets, you will come to realize that the ability to copy and to execute formulas are two of the most powerful tools that spreadsheets offer. However, human beings are still in charge of typing in the formulas, so we must always double-check to make sure that we have told the computer to perform the proper operations. Remember that the computer is only as intelligent as the individual providing the data entry. If we enter the incorrect formula, the computer will not know any better and will perform that function. However, the resulting answer will be skewed and incorrect.
- The third rule in creating an effective spreadsheet relates to something of which you were reminded in both Chapters 10 and 14. If you will recall, we discussed labeling your folders, files, and disks properly. Well, the same approach must be used when creating spreadsheets. The tab at the bottom of the screen allows you to input the name of the sheet. Just as with word processing documents, always give a clear and specific title to your spreadsheet. Make sure that the title accurately describes the contents of the sheet. And, of course, always save your work on a regular basis.
- The fourth rule is not so much a rule as it is a word of advice. Spreadsheets can seem to be very hard to learn, but do not give up because they are worth learning. Once you have mastered this tool, you will be able to produce more attractive documents in half the time that it would take if you use a ruler and calculator.

WHAT ELSE CAN SPREADSHEETS DO?

Right now you are probably feeling overwhelmed and thinking to yourself, "How much more complex can it get?" The good news is that the advanced capabilities of spreadsheets do not become more complex, just more in depth.

Many of the advanced functions that spreadsheets are equipped to perform are statistical in nature, and they *seem* to have little bearing on the life of the typical office worker (i.e., regression analysis, exponential smoothing, etc.). Don't despair, because spreadsheet programs *do* contain mathematical functions that can save you a large amount of time—even if your job description contains no trace of tasks related to financial analysis, regression analysis, or other accounting functions.

The following is a list of some of the other functions that most spreadsheet programs offer:

- finding the average, median, and mode of a set of data;
- calculating sums of sets of data;
- searching through and recovering the highest and lowest values in a data set;
- assigning ordinary numbers specific values in either percentages or dollars; and
- creating color as well as three-dimensional charts and graphs.

The beauty of these functions is that you do not have to input the formula. All you have to do is press one button and the computer does the rest of the work for you. Most spreadsheet programs have a "function" button that you simply click to obtain a list of functions such as adding, averaging, and subtracting. You do not have to execute any complicated commands, nor do you have to develop any formulas. All you have to do is click the right function, and the computer will do the rest. The ease of carrying out these operations can simplify many of the numerous tasks that you usually perform manually. If you are skeptical, simply review the following ordinary tasks:

- reporting the average annual expenditure for health benefits per employee;
- calculating total company income and outgo on a continuing basis;
- identifying the percentage of business expenditures for leasing, supplies, and other expenses;
- computing increases or decreases in salaries, based on employee hiring and firing patterns; and
- calculating the amount of employee time spent in non-work activities.

You can probably add many similar tasks to the above list. Rather than writing the figures on paper, entering them into a calculator, and applying several formula steps, you can leave the work to the spreadsheet software. Given the ease of simply pressing a button to obtain the same or even more accurate results that formerly took hours, you will have more time to organize other areas at work.

HOW CAN SPREADSHEETS SAVE YOU TIME?

Throughout the course of this book we have been showing you ways to save time in your daily routine by increasing your efficiency while never compromising quality. Mastering a spreadsheet program is perhaps the most effective and productive way for you to save time in your daily routine. No longer will you fall victim to miscalculations that can result from hitting the wrong calculator button. For some advanced functions that are common business tasks, you will only have to input one mathematical command, instead of proceeding in the old way in which you would enter each number into a calculator.

Computer-generated spreadsheets also have a more professional and attractive appearance than their handwritten or even typed counterparts. You might not believe that appearance is important, but let's be honest. We all work hard for the money that we earn, but we rarely receive the credit that we deserve for our efforts. If technology can aid us in producing a better-looking product in half the time, why not use it?

In this chapter, we have examined the many ways that using spreadsheets can make you more organized and efficient in the office. As you master each of the areas covered, place a check on the line below:

____ I understand the many uses of spreadsheets.
____ I can identify at least five uses of spreadsheets in my workday.
____ I know the four rules to creating worksheets.
____ I know some of the more advanced functions found in spreadsheet programs.
____ I see how spreadsheets can improve the quality of my work.
____ I find value in the time that using electronic spreadsheets saves me.

Once you can place a check in each of these boxes, you are ready to proceed to the next step in mastering spreadsheets. The next step involves selecting a program and getting acquainted with it. Whereas each person will find different programs comfortable, you should use the one that best interacts with the software used by others in your office. If most of your coworkers use Microsoft Office, then try Excel. If your office uses Lotus as their primary electronic office manager, then use the Lotus spreadsheet program.

Finally, spreadsheet software might *seem* to be a difficult tool to master but the results that you experience will make mastering it worthwhile. Your aim is to get organized, so do not give up. If you become frustrated, walk away for a moment, and then go back. In the end, you will be happy that you took the time to learn to use this tool.

NEXT STEP

In the next chapter, you will learn to use the computer to order online and track purchases, and to use the Internet to save you time and to save your company money.

CHAPTER 17

USING THE INTERNET TO GET ORGANIZED

How much time would you save if you completed a large part of the busywork of business tasks while sitting at your desk? What if you did not have to travel to the office supply store to pick up stationery or supplies? What if you did not even have to sit at your desk holding the telephone receiver and waiting until a customer service representative became available to take your order?

Think of how you could plan and schedule your workday if you knew that you would not have to worry about being interrupted and asked to go to the bank to verify account records or transfer company money. How much better organized could you be if you accessed government statistics via your computer rather than trudging to the library, researching, then copying the information?

If the ability to do all of this and more while seated at your desk and using your computer appeals to you, get ready to go online!

By the end of this chapter, you should be able to do the following:

- Use online search engines to locate product distributors.
- Use bookmarks to return to popular Web sites.
- Understand some of the resources that the Internet offers.
- Track shipments from postal services such as Federal Express and UPS.

WHAT MUST YOU KNOW TO GET STARTED?

Before you can embark on your online journey and use the Internet to organize your office, you must resolve to reorder your thinking regarding cyberspace.

- First, put aside all of your fears and hesitation about using the Internet.
- Second, accept the Internet as an entity that is here to stay, not just some passing fad, and approach the skills that you acquire for working in this area as of lasting value.
- Third, redefine how you function as a consumer and put aside many of the traditional purchasing and tracking methods that you have used in the past.

Do these three prerequisites seem overly simplistic? If they do, they shouldn't. All too often, people perceive the Internet as an evil, undefined force that threatens our way of life. Instead of viewing the Net as an added complication to our lives, we would be far better off if we viewed it as a tool designed to make life easier. Indeed, the depth and breadth of the Internet are quite vast and confusing, but that does not mean you cannot harness the usefulness of specific areas that are helpful to you.

Have you avoided the Internet because you don't understand it? An analogy can be made between breathing and your interaction with the Internet. Every second of every day you inhale oxygen and exhale carbon dioxide, right? We all do, but few among us could actually explain in accurate medical and biological detail the internal workings of this process. Yet although we are not able to explain *how* our bodies effectively process air, we continue to breathe every second of the day. In the same way, you do not need to understand how everything on the Internet functions to make use of it.

To get organized at work by accessing the Internet, you need the same equipment that you needed to use e-mail: a computer, a modem, communications software, a telephone line, and an Internet provider (America Online, Compuserve, Prodigy, AT&T, or a number of others).

Once you are online, several organizing tools make searching and communicating on the Internet more manageable, including search engines and bookmarks.

Search Engines

Imagine the Internet as a library full of information. Whether you would like to know the latest score in the Yankees vs. Mets baseball game, the present form of a piece of legislation that is being considered by a Senate committee, or the best prices in office supplies, the Internet has that information. In a physical library, you would be wasting time if you walked through each row of shelves looking for a book that interests you, or hoping to find, by chance, a book that relates to the topic that you have in mind. To avoid this waste of time, libraries have card or computer catalogs. To prevent people from wasting their time when they are looking for information on the Internet, search engines exist to use for locating sources.

Despite its relatively impressive name, a search engine is an address or a doorway to the Internet that allows you to type in topics about which you want more information. Each of the premium provider services has its own form of search engine. In addition, several others can also be accessed by typing in their addresses or by going to their sites. For Yahoo, type in *http://www.yahoo.com*, and for AltaVista, the address is *http://www.altavista.com*. You can obtain the names and site addresses of others by simply typing in the words "search engine" in some provider programs, and just follow directions for others.

How can you use these search engines? Let's assume, for example, that you wish to compare the prices of office supplies from various companies, so that you can reduce costs and increase your convenience in ordering. A large number of companies of all types have Web sites and offer online ordering. You could go to the search engine, type in the phrase "office supplies," and the engine, or *browser* as it is sometimes also called, will return to you a listing of other Web sites that will give you more information.

These search engines allow you to become a more competitive shopper. Instead of maintaining your company's association with one distributor who may not charge the lowest prices, you can now get a listing of other distributors. Before access to so many companies on the Internet became possible, you had to look in the commercial (yellow) pages of the telephone directory, call each office supplier, wait for them to mail you their catalogs, and then finally make your purchasing decisions by mail or by telephone. Using search engines allows you to get the same comparative shopping information in a matter of minutes, where it would have previously taken days to gather the same pricing information.

Bookmarks

Isn't it annoying to have to type in the exact address for a Web site each time you want to visit it? Furthermore, what happens if you lose the sticky note on which you wrote the site address? Most Internet services provide a feature called a "bookmark," designed to deal with just such a situation.

Bookmarks, like their physical counterparts, allow a computer user to save a place—in this case, a favorite Web site. After typing in the site address, you can just click a button on what is called "favorite places" on America Online (and given different names on others), and the computer will save that Web site address. The next time that you wish to visit the site, all you have to do is click on the bookmark option on your screen, then select the name of the exact page, and the computer will automatically take you there. This is much easier than typing in those long Web addresses—or trying to locate a sticky note with a Web address on it that may be buried under a stack of files and papers.

WHAT CAN THE WEB DO FOR YOU?

The services offered on the Internet are indeed quite vast, but there seem to be about four ways that it can directly help to organize any business and save you time. The first is through comparative shopping, the second is facilitated ordering, the third is online tracking, and the fourth is research access. These four services have been selected for discussion because they are of interest to every business and every office. Note, however, that many other services that may suit the needs of specific businesses are also offered on the Internet and should be explored by the reader.

Comparative Shopping

Let's say that your boss comes to you and instructs you to book him one round-way airplane ticket going from Miami to New York City. Company profits have not been as high this quarter, and cutbacks have been made in the travel budget, so he wants you to locate the lowest price airfare that you can and book him a flight.

Normally, you would place telephone calls to a host of airlines and travel agents until you found the lowest price. However, now that you have access to the Internet, you no longer need to go through this hassle. Instead of picking up the phone, you switch on the computer and type in something like "cheap airline tickets" into your search engine. The computer spits out a number of different Web sites, and you select one. Once on this particular site you enter the proper information into the computer, such as destination and departure and arrival dates, and the computer gives you a listing of prices and flights for different airlines.

In only five minutes you will have accomplished what would have normally taken you one or two hours. Furthermore, you did not have to deal with the aggravation of being put on hold, or of waiting while the reservation agent found the best rate.

The attraction of the Internet is that you are not limited to shopping for office supplies and airplane tickets. This resource also allows its searchers to shop for almost any item or good in the world. In addition, it gives you up-to-date price quotes without having to wait for the company's catalog or newsletter to arrive in the mail. The following is only a partial list of other goods and services for which you can shop on the Internet:

- books,
- rental cars,
- hotel reservations,
- computers,
- suits,
- contracting services,
- flowers, and
- groceries.

The list is vast and continues to grow as a greater number of companies establish their Web sites. In the end, basically any good or service that you can think of will be found on the Internet. Many of these companies do not need to pay for things such as paper on which to print their advertising, nor do they have the overhead costs of an extra office and floor space. These lower expenses allow companies that appear on the Internet to offer the consumer discounted prices. Not only can comparative shopping on the Internet save you time, but it could also save your company money.

Online Ordering

Not only does the Internet allow you to shop around for the best prices without ever picking up the telephone, but it also allows you to place orders in the same way.

Let's return to the earlier example of making an airline reservation through the Internet. After checking for the best airline deal, you may have found a super low price on a great airline that will offer your boss comfort and still save money. Now, you want to make certain that you can book a reservation on that flight.

Go to the airline's Web site, where, most likely, the Web page will instruct you how to order the tickets. In most cases, you will have to make some sort of payment, either through a personal credit card or through a corporate account, depending on the service and the company. When you reach the site, you will read a message assuring you that security software is in use to protect your credit card number, then you will be prompted to enter the company credit card number into the account. At the directive, you will press the "okay" button and wait. After a few seconds you will see a new screen appear to confirm your reservation. This screen usually includes important information that you will need to use the ticket, to correct an error if the ticket reservation is somehow corrupted, or to confirm the reservation in advance, just to be sure. Have a pen and paper ready to write down the confirmation number, date and time of the flight, from which gate the flight will leave, and a host of other information. Or, take the smarter and easier route and, instead of writing all of this information down, you can click on the print button and your computer will print out a copy of the confirmation information. Ordering online makes your life a little easier. It provides you with a way of organizing your time because you can plan when and how long you will search, and it helps to bring you into the information age.

Tracking Your Purchases

The Internet also offers a way for you to track the delivery of the purchases that you have made and the packages that you have sent.

Let's look at an example of how you might use the Internet to track a package sent by the company you work for.

Let's pretend that your company is a wholesale supplier of flowers to florists. Last Tuesday, you shipped a box of unusually delicate flowers to a client in Butte, Montana, using a nationwide shipping service. You have still not received a telephone call or e-mail message from that client to acknowledge receipt of the flowers, so you should assume that the flowers have not yet arrived. Still, the length of time that has passed is unusual, and you decide to check on the shipment in the most common way at present. To follow up, you call the shipping company, where a representative gives you the telephone number of their regional office. When you call the regional office, a representative tells you to call customer service, where you are given yet another telephone number to call, and so on and so on. Does this never-ending trail of phone numbers sound familiar to you? This runaround can become frustrating very quickly, and many times it offers little in the way of results.

Is there anything else that you can do? Many shipping companies offer an alternative to these endless phone calls. Major shipping companies have now developed online tracking software that you can install on your personal computer. This software connects with their computers and allows you to see the status of your shipment. The software is a free service offered by the company, and the peace of mind that it offers will cost you and your company absolutely nothing.

So, let's revisit our scenario. Instead of calling the shipping company, you log onto their Web site or open your tracking software. Next, you key in your shipping code. The computer then tells you that the package actually did arrive yesterday at 4:52 p.m. and that a Mr. John Doe signed for it.

Research Access

Let's move our attention away from goods consumerism and toward information consumerism. We will examine how the Internet can spare you hours of time spent in a library, poring over files, government reports and pamphlets, and newspapers.

The growth in interest in the Internet has been accompanied by an increase in the number of organizations and government agencies that have created Web sites and made extensive information available. You can print out case studies and profiles of various countries, compliments of the Central Intelligence Agency (CIA), or locate and print out a copy of current legislation that may still be in Senate committee, compliments of the Library of Congress. Many government agencies provide data, such as the Bureau of Labor Statistics and the Bureau of the Census, which regularly update their statistics. You can identify their addresses by the extension ".gov", as opposed to the extensions used by commercial sites (".com"), educational or university sites (".edu"), or organization sites (".org").

To access research sites, use the same approach that you used to locate goods and services. Locate a search engine and simply type in the topic in which you are interested. Then bookmark the sites to which you expect to make repeat visits.

What type of information might your company ask you to research? Legislation affects different industries at different times. You boss may have learned of a bill still in committee that proposes to limit import of a specific item that may be used in manufacturing your company's main money-making item. In the past, he would send you to a nearby library, local or university, to look through the magazine index, back issues of newspapers, and copies of *The Congressional Record*. Now, you can go to the Internet to locate information—if not the full text, then at least summaries that will tell where the material is located.

The library in the town in which your company is located may also be online as part of a consortium of libraries that share resources. The policy of many town libraries is to extend borrowing privileges to the executives and their designees of companies that do business in the town, even if they live outside of the town. To learn how you can access magazine and newspaper articles and even print them out on your office computer, call the town library director. Your courtesy privileges can be valuable in helping you to access data.

The true beauty of all these services is that they make your life easier. Learning the techniques of surfing the Internet may be an initially cumbersome task, but gaining proficiency will save you a great amount of time. Do you remember what we said in the previous chapter about spreadsheets? They may be hard to master initially, but once you can master that tool, you will save yourself vast amounts of time. The same can be said for learning to access sites on the Internet. Once you gain an understanding of how the Internet can help you and your business, it will save you both time and money. You will find that you will have more time to plan and to schedule other activities, and you will become more organized in the process.

You have identified several important ways that using the Internet can be valuable for you and enhance your workday experience. As you master each step, place a check on the line below:

____ I no longer view the Internet as a threat, rather as another tool to facilitate my work.
____ I understand the uses and powers of search engines.
____ I know how to bookmark Web sites to save time and effort.

____ I understand the universal applications of shopping, purchasing, and tracking products on the Web.

____ I am comfortable locating government and other statistical data on the Web.

NEXT STEP

In this chapter, you have identified ways of locating and using search engines, bookmarking Web sites, and accessing information from the Internet. In the next section, you will identify the types of records and information that can be purged from paper and computer files, and you will examine ways of disposing of such information.

SECTION V

MERGING AND PURGING INFORMATION

Most of the discussion of how to get organized at work has focused on how to save time and to eliminate needless effort by using the equipment and techniques that will make us most efficient. In the chapters that discussed filing, we spoke of eliminating duplication and of sorting out the necessary from the unnecessary information, but the focus was largely on active files. Concern with purging and merging is also a part of the discussion in other chapters that focus on combining tasks and working more efficiently as you complete your workday tasks.

What we have not discussed are the guidelines for deciding what stays and what goes among archival files. How long should you keep employee health insurance records? What effect does the statute of limitations have on retaining records of different types of insurance coverage? How long should your company keep pension plan records? Should tax records be kept forever? Which records to save and which to throw out—and when—are important to the effective organization and functioning of a company?

This section identifies necessary records and provides you with time guidelines for how long certain records must be kept. Also important to effectively maintaining records is knowing how to purge records and various means of safe disposal. You may have few or no decisions to make regarding many of the company records. Accountants and others whom the company may have on retainer should make decisions regarding financial and legal records. Nonetheless, you should also know the guidelines for keeping or tossing records, if only as a check against mistakes that others might make.

CHAPTER 18

RETAINING AND REMOVING RECORDS

Most companies keep as many years of records as the amount of space available for their storage. Paper copies, computer disks, hard-drive backups, and even microfilm all share popularity as means of storing financial, legal, and other records.

The extent to which records accrue and take up space depends on the size of a company, the complexity of the corporate structure, the number of its sites, and other factors over which you have no control. If you work for a company of even moderate size, you may not even have any control over which records to keep and which to toss. In contrast, if you work for a small company, the burden of making these decisions may be mainly yours.

Even if your duties consist of maintaining the files and only following the directives of others when the time comes to merge and purge files, this chapter will be helpful to you. Others can make mistakes, and they may direct you to carry out their mistakes. If your responsibilities even to a small extent include maintaining files, then the possibility is strong that, at some point, you will have to make a decision whether to save or to toss files. Now is the time to identify the guidelines of this task—not when you are rushed to make a decision or to carry out someone else's.

WHAT IS YOUR ROLE IN COMPANY RECORD KEEPING?

The threat of an audit by the Internal Revenue Service leads many companies to become obsessive about their financial record keeping. That's a valid concern, but even without this threat, companies should maintain accurate, long-term financial records as a means of charting progress and providing a financial history.

You might be wondering what this has to do with you if you simply draw a paycheck and have no say in the management of the company. As you have already learned in earlier chapters in this book, many of your *seemingly* minor duties do have important implications for the company, but the isolated manner in which you and your coworkers may be expected to work hides this connection.

You have already responded to several checklists that were used to identify the tasks for which you are responsible at work. Many of these tasks, especially those connected to reorganizing the filing system, have an effect on the accuracy and effectiveness of the company financial records. Take a moment and check off all of the following tasks that you have been asked to complete. Several tasks are grouped within most of the items to keep the checklist within a reasonable length. Even if you have only typed or filed correspondence related to one type of employee concern listed in the item, check it. Use the same judgment in regard to items that ask if you handled several types of records.

Records-Related Task Checklist

____ Typed or filed tax records and documents to submit to the accounting department or to an outside accounting firm.

____ Typed or filed correspondence or documents related to employee health benefits, pension records, or personnel records.

____ Typed or filed correspondence or documents related to company profits or company losses.

____ Typed or filed correspondence or documents related to employee business expense declarations.

____ Typed or filed correspondence or documents related to the appreciation or depreciation of equipment.

____ Typed or filed correspondence or documents related to the appreciation or depreciation of buildings.

____ Typed or filed correspondence or documents related to company property taxes.

____ Typed or filed correspondence or documents related to the collection of sales tax by the company.

____ Typed or filed correspondence or documents related to company payment of withholding and Social Security taxes.

How many of the nine items above did you check? If you have only performed one of the tasks—either typing or filing of a letter or other document connected to the financial side of the company—then you have played a role in the financial future of the company.

Why consider this? Despite our feelings that we have no role in some functions of a company, many of our tasks do have the potential to affect its success or failure.

Consider the following:

- How would your accuracy in typing or filing documents related to employee business expenses change the deductions declared by your company accountant in a given tax year?
- What would happen in a tax audit of your company for the year 1996 if you had accidentally purged the paper and computer files related to 1996 business losses—instead of the records for 1976, as you might have been instructed to do?
- What are the chances that your company will obtain a loan to expand its facilities if they cannot locate profit and loss statements for significant years that you misfiled or lost?

As you see, the tasks that you routinely perform can have a great effect on the financial future of your company. Even if you are careful in completing all of the above tasks, others may direct you to remove or to destroy many of these records either sporadically or on a regular basis to save space and to weed out seemingly worthless or outdated information. The more knowledgeable that you are regarding which records to keep and the length of time to keep them, the less likely it is that you will compound the errors of others.

WHAT ARE YOUR GUIDELINES FOR KEEPING RECORDS?

The length of time to keep records may vary slightly, according to the type of record, but most guidelines for financial records remain relatively consistent from year to year.

Annual Tax Records

In general, you should keep all of the records that support the declarations and deductions appearing on the company income tax documents. These items are more numerous than those that we keep for our personal income tax records.

Which company records should you keep to support annual tax records? Keep all proof of deductible expenses, including receipts, canceled checks, automobile mileage and use logs, and 1099 statements (client reimbursements, royalties, and dividends). If the company included any unusual calculations or entries on tax returns in a given year, save all of the notes and other information that document the reasons for discrepancies or other unusual circumstances and place them with the specific return. Your company records should also save cancelled checks, wire transfer statements, and other bank or financial statements. To prove that the company has made its estimated tax payments as required, save the canceled checks for these payments and place them with the tax records for the same year.

Past Tax Returns

Keep all of the company tax returns and the supporting documents for the history of the company. These records provide a concise annual record of the financial life of the company.

Personnel Records

These records provide a history of the hiring and firing activities of your company, as well as financial information that is useful to both the company and its current and past employees. Such records contain individual data regarding employee salaries, in addition to the withholding, Social Security, and income taxes that both the employee and the company paid. Keeping these records is important to maintaining the company's financial history, but it may also be important for a past employee who may require such information to verify income to collect Social Security payments or for other reasons.

Pension Records

Certainly, the importance of these records might seem obvious to any employee who looks forward to a reasonably comfortable retirement, but what must be kept? If the company has a 401(k) plan, keep all employee pension records, as well as the plan documents and the annual statements of all transactions provided by the bank, broker, or mutual fund company that administers the plan.

Equipment Depreciation and Deduction Records

Receipts and canceled checks for all equipment are routinely kept to document purchases and to support warranty information. When these receipts are also used to verify tax deductions that your company may take, they acquire new meaning. Because the information will be used for two purposes, this is one time that duplicate copies of receipts should be made and filed in all appropriate areas.

Profit and Loss Statements

Records of profit and loss provide a financial history of the company that can be used to analyze the successful or not-so-successful operation of the business. You may not be too interested in seeing how well the company did in the years before present management took over, but such information is important if the company were to apply for a loan to expand its operations. Profit and loss statements are also used to appraise the market value of a company, so all of the company's statements would be reviewed if the owner decided to sell the company. Incomplete records would have a severe negative effect on the credibility of the ownership.

Loss Records

Documenting company losses, such as equipment write-offs or other deductions, is extremely important, and these records can prove useful for more than just a current year. Depending on changes in the tax codes, your company might be able to carry net operating losses back three years, which can be valuable should the IRS audit the company tax returns for one, two, or three previous years and if further deductions must be established. These same loss records can also be carried *forward* 15 years, so if your company may not be able to take a deduction now, it may want to use these records to offset profits 10 or more years from now.

Nonessential Records

Can you throw out anything? Despite the seemingly endless list of records that you must keep for long periods of time, you will find many records to purge. Insurance policies that are no longer in force, equipment warranties and extended service plans that have expired, registration cards for equipment either no longer in use or no longer owned, letters of reference from other employers for employees no longer with the company, and petty cash receipts should all be purged.

Records are important, and many—but not all—should be kept for the life of the company. Can you purge anything from the company files? A lot still remains that is nonessential. When we discussed organizing your company files (Chapter 10), we identified quite a few types of reference and archive files that *should* be merged and even purged on a regular basis, as well as active files that you should scrutinize carefully. Review that chapter to identify which files to toss.

Use the following list of records and the *minimum* length of time they should be retained as only a guide. For more specific information, follow the advice of the company accountant and legal experts.

RECORDS REVIEW LIST

If you find that your company has records that do not appear on the list below, check with your manager or a legal expert to make certain that you keep every record for the correct length of time.

Type Of Record	*Minimum Time To Keep*
Financial records:	
Annual income tax records	7 years
Annual income tax return forms	Forever
Bank statements	7 years
Contracts (non-rental)	7 years after arrangement ends
Loan agreements	7 years after repayment is complete

Documents supporting loss	7 years after last deduction is used
Pension plan records (employee data)	Forever
Pension plan records (transactions)	7 years
Personnel records (unemployment taxes, Social Security, and other related data)	7 years after the employee has left the company
Profit and loss statements	Forever
Rental and leasing contracts	7 years
Sales records	7 years after sale is finalized

Insurance records:

Automobile	Statute of limitations*
Business property	Statute of limitations*
Disability (employee)	7 years after policy ends
Health and medical (employee)	7 years after policy ends
Liability	Statute of limitations*
Umbrella	7 years after policy ends

Miscellaneous records:

Automobile registration	1 year after sold or donated
Business equipment (receipts)	7 years after last used as tax deduction
Improvements to physical plant (contracts, receipts)	7 years after used as tax deduction OR 7 years after property is sold
Mortgage records	7 years after property is sold
Warranties	As long as company owns items

*The statute of limitations varies, so check with state requirements.

NEXT STEP

This chapter examined the types of records that a company might keep and identified the length of time each record should be kept. In the next chapter, you will consider ways to dispose safely of unnecessary records and files.

CHAPTER 19

DESTROYING FILES SAFELY

Getting organized at work requires knowing what to throw out as well as what to keep. In Section III, when you examined ways to organize your desk and the area surrounding it, you learned that an important means of making that area more efficient is to discard unnecessary paper, equipment, and supplies. For the most part, however, much of what you might discard from your desk and bookshelves has no informational value. Material that you might have kept piled on your desk and later cleaned off should not raise issues of confidentiality if thrown out. Your scraps of paper and files should not relate to personal employee information nor to confidential workings of the company, because such files should always be carefully secured. If you do have such files lying about, then you might be violating company policies and leaving important material unguarded. Review your actions to protect yourself and your company from prying eyes.

WHICH FILES ARE IMPORTANT?

Once you have determined that files and other information are no longer useful to the company—or once you have been given the directive to clean out files or other depositories of information, you have to make a decision about how to dispose of the material. You might feel that the trash can is good enough, feeling that if your company no longer wants the information, why would anyone else? That type of thinking is a mistake, and how big a mistake it might be depends on the type of work that your company does. As taxpayers, we are often surprised to learn of small companies with apparently mundane products that are under contract with the government to manufacture important parts or to conduct obscure but vital laboratory research. Even if the connection between your company and another, or between your company and the government, has not been as mysterious nor as exciting as suggested here, some information in any company's files is best left secret.

You may call such thinking paranoia, but you might be more understanding of the concerns of a company if you would imagine for a moment how you would feel if an old address book of yours became public knowledge. How would you feel—and how would the people listed in the book feel—if long-forgotten names and other data were to be seen by strangers? What if it were seen by people who knew you and those listed? Even if nothing humiliating were written, you would still feel violated to a certain degree. Most of us would.

Companies have a lot more to lose—and a once-flourishing business partnership can become an embarrassment a decade later. People who worked for the company may not want their personnel folders, with all of the personal data that might be included, scattered for others to read. Company reports, bank statements, contracts, loan agreements, mortgage arrangements, pension plan transactions, and other records may be completely irrelevant to the present management and even the present corporate structure. Nevertheless, somewhere in such information might lurk embarrassing facts or figures. For these and many other reasons, any records or data that are purged from company files should be permanently disposed of. *How* you do so, however, depends on the resources available in your company.

HOW SHOULD YOU DISPOSE OF FILES?

Some old-fashioned methods of destroying records, such as burning them, have become impractical in the multistory office buildings that contain smoke alarms and sprinkler systems—which may entail an elevator ride down 50 floors to reach the boiler room. Instead, companies today use a variety of means to dispose of useless files: recycling, throwing them into the trash can, shredding, erasing, and reformatting. Each approach has its advantages, and the nature and the quantity of the material being purged should determine the means of disposal.

Recycling

A large company with many office personnel and the potential for large quantities of paper to recycle each week might forge its own agreement with a recycling company. As an example, Marcal Paper Products, located in Elmwood Park, New Jersey, receives regular deliveries of paper for recycling from the local school district and other school districts. The company prides itself on being an industry leader in recycling. Lumber companies and manufacturers of paper products throughout the United States do the same. Companies that don't have access to such a plant, or companies that have few employees, might simply take their "safe" paper to the local town recycling site or leave it for pickup in the lobby if their office building has its own recycling program. Be careful that the files and documents you recycle are those that do not contain important company information and nothing of a confidential nature.

Throwing in the Trash

Small quantities of files and papers that are of little informational value can be thrown into the trash can and left for the scheduled garbage pickup, if no recycling program is available. Such papers should be "safe" and they should not contain personal employee information nor confidential business agreements or financial data.

Shredding

You might feel that shredding would be the most effective way of disposing of files and papers that contain sensitive data, but this approach is not always foolproof. For example, when the U.S. embassy in Iran was forced to hurriedly evacuate American diplomats nearly two decades ago, office workers were ordered to shred all of the files that they had to leave behind. In the weeks that followed, U.S. newspapers carried stories and photographs of Iranians painstakingly sorting through the shredded papers and attempting to reconstruct documents. One hopeful note in this story is that no follow-up stories emerged to state that anything of importance had actually been reconstructed.

Unless your company is the target of high-level industrial sabotage or part of a top-secret government project, shredding the purged documents should be effective. If your company does not own a shredder, suggest that management authorize the purchase of one for your office. Most office supply stores sell different sizes, from those with a six-inch feed-in to those with an 11-inch feed-in, for under $100, including the size-matched wastebasket.

Erasing

Just as the approaches of recycling and shredding apply only to the disposal of purged paper files, "erasing" refers to the disposal of information contained on disks, tape backups, hard drives, and the more recently marketed writable CDs. You might feel that simply throwing the disks, tapes, and CDs into the trash might be sufficient, but it is not. If rival companies or media snoops want to obtain information about your company, they will find ways to read your disks and tapes, no matter how different your equipment and software might be from theirs. A determined individual will find an expert to use "bridge" software that will convert files to a readable format.

You should also know that even erasing files from disks and tapes is not enough to protect your company from pirating—not if the information on these items is very confidential or very damaging to your company's image and not if someone wants it badly enough. Computer experts have aided law enforcement agencies in raising images from erased videotapes and raised sounds from erased audiotapes. They have also managed to recover fairly complete files from computer disks and CDs that people thought they had carefully erased. What many people, even those proficient with computers, may not know or perhaps forget is that many computer programs automatically insert an "unformat" command on a disk to protect users against accidentally wiping out files. Even if that doesn't exist, computer disks and CDs also may not erase completely. Instead, either chunks of information may remain at different places on the disk or CD, or faint "writing" may still exist, which can be recovered by the powerful equipment used by a computer expert.

To be honest, you and your company probably have little to worry about, because what is recovered usually contains "holes" or gaps in the material. Still, if enough information has been raised from presumably erased disks to be used in the courtroom, might other computer experts recover enough of your files to reveal company secrets or to embarrass management and employees?

Only a few companies may worry to such a great extent about their purged files. You may not even know how important secrecy regarding certain files is to management in your company. Still, you should be aware that you must do more than erase files if your company absolutely has to feel secure. In addition to erasing the information, you also have to destroy the media.

If retaining confidentiality is of extreme importance, then after erasing files, also do the following:

- Cut open each erased diskette and use sharp scissors to cut into small pieces the black flexible disk inside. Scatter the pieces among different trash bags.
- Cut each erased tape in half lengthwise, then cut the two long strips into small pieces. Scatter the pieces among different trash bags.
- Smash or cut each erased CD into small pieces. Scatter the pieces among different trash bags.
- Ask your manager to bring in an expert to erase and to reformat the computer hard drive. If the concern is so great as to be worth the cost, then replace the hard drive. Erase then destroy the old hard drive, as in the above items.

Most of us just want to complete our jobs competently and efficiently. Few of us are aware of the intrigue or secrets that take place at the highest levels in our companies—and most of us probably don't care. However, if you are given the responsibility to purge files and to destroy them, you would be wise to ask for clear and specific directions from your supervisor.

Among the questions that you should ask are the following:

- Who has authorized or signed off on the project?
- Will you receive your instructions in writing, in a memo that lists the types of files that you are to purge and the range of dates?
- Does the company require a certain means of disposal?
- Are any of the files of a "sensitive" nature?

NEXT STEP

This chapter reviewed the various approaches to purging outdated, no longer needed files and provided suggestions for effective file and document disposal. In the final chapter, you will review the pitfalls of getting organized at work that confront even the most motivated individuals.

SECTION | VI

STAYING ORGANIZED

Reaching the goal of getting organized at work can take a lot of work, and you are not really finished even after you have achieved all the changes that we discuss throughout this book. Despite your best intentions, you will eventually be tempted to allow file folders to pile up on your desk and to use pushpins to post piles of notes and telephone numbers on your bulletin board.

When that happens, you should think about all the work that you have put into organizing your desk environment and files. You know that you will have an easier time staying organized if you vow to clear the clutter at the end of each workday, rather than wait until the mess is so bad that you can't see your desk.

What can you do if you find yourself becoming disorganized, once again? You know how hard you worked to become better organized at work, so don't let moments of weakness undermine all that you have accomplished. When you need help, use some of the techniques for staying organized that you will find in Chapter 20.

CHAPTER | 20

MAINTENANCE TIPS FOR STAYING ORGANIZED AT WORK

Getting organized is not easy, but *staying* organized can be even more difficult. You should enjoy the feelings of control and self-confidence that you gain from being organized, but little difficulties can cause you to backslide. Prepare in advance for the occasional slip, so nothing will catch you by surprise.

HOW CAN YOU KEEP YOUR SYSTEM WORKING?

To keep yourself organized, plan regular maintenance periods to assess how your system is working. You devised this system, so you should also be the person to make any changes that might be needed as your responsibilities change or your work life changes.

How often should you schedule these maintenance periods? Every week? Every month? Every six months? The frequency of your checkups depends on how well the system continues to work. You don't have to plan anything elaborate, just a question-and-answer session with yourself in which you respond honestly to the following:

- How is my system working?
- Where and how is it breaking down (if at all)?
- What can I do to improve my system?
- What have I learned?
- How can I streamline this system, or make it more efficient and save even more time?

To make your maintenance checkup more effective, make an appointment with yourself to evaluate and plan any needed changes. Don't just wait until your desk area has again become cluttered with stacks of papers or until files are spilling out of the "in" and "out" boxes.

If you establish a regular time slot during which you review how well you have maintained your organization, then you will be more likely to keep your promise to yourself to remain organized. During these appointments with yourself, you should review the original mission, goals, and plans, and decide if your goals have changed in any way. If so, then you might wish to add something more to your planning. You should continue to develop your system. When you think of another idea or if you change or add a goal, write it down, then think about adding the idea or goal to your system.

HOW CAN COWORKERS HELP?

A variation on the old saying that your personal behavior will be influenced by your friends is also true in regard to staying organized at work. You will be more likely to return to your inefficient and disorganized ways if you associate with coworkers who refuse to tackle this problem. Instead of letting these coworkers drag you down again, build a new network of positive thinkers—organized and motivated achievers who take pride in their work and who make others' and their own lives better.

If you can't change your office associations because of small office size, or if such a change is not desirable, then try to make the people who refuse to change at least understand that *you* have changed—and that you like the change. When you speak with them, explain your mission and your goals.

What should you do if they refuse to accept your change? Well, what would you do if they refused to accept a specific moral principle in which you believe, or if they refused to include a friend of yours in a social gathering? Would you let other people regulate your moral thinking or your friendships? I doubt that you would. So, don't allow their disapproval to destroy the success that you have achieved.

Even as you associate with the old network, look around and find models for success who have solved the problems that you are working hard to solve. Study what they do and how they do it. Seeing others who can maintain a higher standard at work will motivate you, as well.

WHAT CAN YOU DO IF YOUR SYSTEM STOPS WORKING?

Before your system has a chance to break down, accept the reality that it is bound to do so at some point. Also, resolve that you will not simply abandon all that you have achieved if it should start to fail. Instead, you will apply your problem-solving skills to analyzing where the problem lies and to identifying what you must do to make the system begin functioning once again.

Should problems arise, review what you have been doing and determine if you have been trying to do too much. To correct this, select one task to do well and completely. Focus your complete attention on the task so that you can achieve your goal. Then select another task, and complete it in the same thorough way.

You have to re-establish your sense of control, and the only way to do that is by concentrating on one area and mastering it again before attempting to do more.

Once you have regained an element of control, assess what went wrong. Don't look at the big picture immediately. Instead, examine one day at a time and review how each day is working—or why it is not working. You will find that your system will still work on some days, but it will not work on others. Methodically ask yourself the following questions in the "Getting Organized Maintenance Checkup" on page 178, and be very honest in your answers.

After you have assessed why your system of organization broke down on a given day, take steps to prevent that from occurring again. Were other people the problem? Were *you* the problem? Did you simply have too much work to complete in too short a time?

If your plan needs fine-tuning, then work on it and rewrite or reorganize it, but don't give up. You don't have to be perfect—just organized.

If you find that your difficulties arise on different days, but not continuously, examine what occurs during those days to disrupt your system. You deserve to

Getting Organized Maintenance Checkup

Date of the day assessed_____

1. Did problems occur? If so, what were the problems?
   _____
   _____
   _____
   _____

2. How could I have prevented or solved the problems?
   _____
   _____
   _____
   _____

3. Are the problems in areas that I have already addressed—or are they new?
   _____
   _____
   _____
   _____

4. Did the problems occur because I am overburdened with work?
   _____
   _____
   _____
   _____

5. Would delegating some of my responsibility to others help?
   _____
   _____
   _____
   _____

achieve success at work, and getting organized is the way to succeed. Post the following "Rules for Staying Organized" somewhere that only you can see them, and read them every day. Even on bad days, you will find something in the list to get you back on track. Good luck in maintaining your newfound feelings of control.

Rules For Staying Organized

- DO force yourself to focus.
- DO instruct yourself to work.
- DO tell people that you are busy working.
- DO reorganize when the system seems to fail.
- DO concentrate on one area at a time.
- DO master the system—don't let it master you.
- DO ask others for help when you need it.
- DO remind yourself how being organized gives you a pleasant sense of being in control.
- DO avoid procrastination.
- DO reward yourself for your hard work.

APPENDIX

ADDITIONAL RESOURCES

Are you ready to get organized? You may feel that you need a little more help in a particular area. The following books will provide tips on specific skills and applications.

Brooks, Lloyd D. *101 Spreadsheet Exercises* (Macmillan/McGraw Hill, 1992).

Chesla, Elizabeth. *Improve Your Writing for Work: The Basics Made Easy* (LearningExpress, 1997.)

Farrell, Thomas J. *Effective Telephone Skills* (Dryden Press, 1994).

Fox, Grace. *Office Etiquette and Protocol: The Basics Made Easy* (LearningExpress, 1998).

Ginn, Mary Lea. *Easy Filing With Microcomputer Applications* (South-Western, 1992).

Gold, Gloria. *How to Set Up and Implement a Records Management System* (AMACOM, 1995).

Heller, Bernard. *The 100 Most Difficult Business Letters You'll Ever Have to Write, Fax, or E-Mail* (HarperBusiness, 1994).

Margolis, Andrew. *The Fax Modem Source Book* (John Wiley & Sons, 1995).

Rankin, Bob. *Dr. Bob's Painless Guide to the Internet: & Amazing Things You Can Do With E-Mail* (No Starch Press, 1996).

MASTER THE BASICS ... FAST!
WITH THE EXCLUSIVE LEARNINGEXPRESS ADVANTAGE

These books are for you if need to improve your basic skills to move ahead, either at work or in the classroom.
- Become a Better Student—**Quickly**
- Become a More Marketable Employee—**Fast**
- Get a Better Job—**Now**

Specifically Designed for Classroom Learning OR Independent Home Study!
- 20 easy-to-follow lessons build confidence and skill FAST
- Focus on real-world skills—what you REALLY need to succeed in school and on the job
- Dozens of exercises, hundreds of practical tips, and easy-to-implement steps to SUCCESS

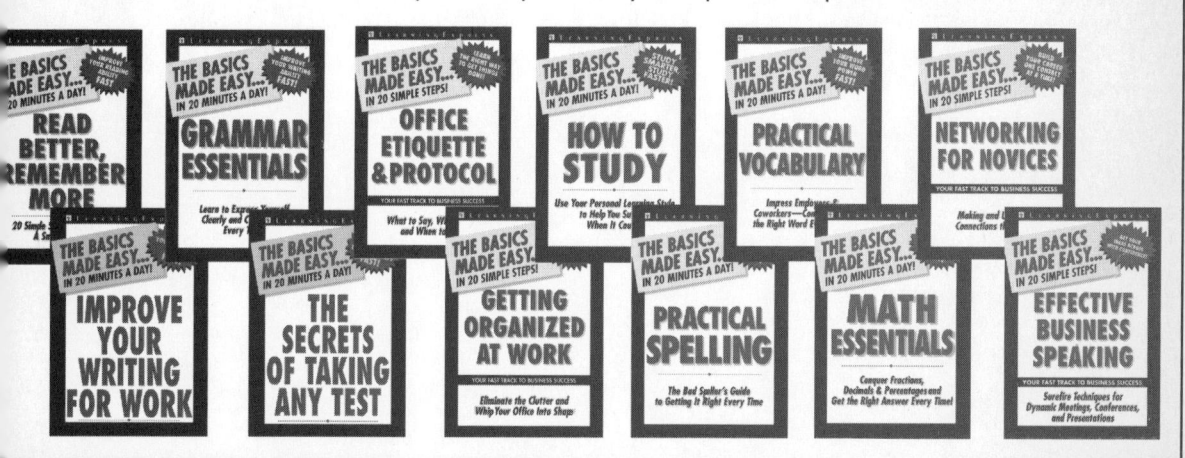

___ READ BETTER, REMEMBER MORE	Item #060-9	___ HOW TO STUDY	Item# 084-6
___ IMPROVE YOUR WRITING FOR WORK	Item #061-7	___ PRACTICAL SPELLING	Item #083-8
___ GRAMMAR ESSENTIALS	Item #062-5	___ PRACTICAL VOCABULARY	Item #082-X
___ THE SECRETS OF TAKING ANY TEST	Item #071-4	___ MATH ESSENTIALS	Item #094-3
___ OFFICE ETIQUETTE & PROTOCOL	Item #145-1	___ NETWORKING FOR NOVICES	Item #143-5
___ GETTING ORGANIZED AT WORK	Item #144-3	___ EFFECTIVE BUSINESS SPEAKING	Item #146-X

SPECIFICATIONS: 7 x 10 • 208–224 PAGES • $13.95 EACH (PAPERBACK)

ORDER THE BASICS MADE EASY YOU NEED TODAY:
Fill in the quantities beside each book and mail your check or money order*
for the amount indicated (please include $6.95 postage & handling
for the first book and $1.00 for each additional book) to:

LearningExpress, Dept. A040, 20 Academy Street, Norwalk, CT 06850
Or call, TOLL-FREE: **1-888-551-JOBS**, Dept. A040 to place a credit card order.
Also available in your local bookstores

ase allow at least 2-4 weeks for delivery. Prices subject to change without notice   *NY, CT, & MD residents add appropriate sales tax

LEARNINGEXPRESS®
An Affiliate Company of Random House, Inc.

LEARNINGEXPRESS

AT LAST—
Test Preparation that REALLY Works

IMPROVE YOUR SCORES WITH THE EXCLUSIVE LEARNINGEXPRESS ADVANTAGE!

Competition for top jobs is tough. You need all the advantages you can get. That's why LearningExpress has created easy-to-use test prep and career guides, many *customized* specifically for the high-demand jobs in your city and state.

Only LearningExpress gives:

- Exclusive practice exams based on official tests given in specific cities and states
- Hundreds of sample questions with answers & explanations by experts
- Key contacts, salaries & application procedures for individual cities

Plus:

- Unique LearningExpress Exam Planners
- Critical skill-building exercises in reading comprehension, math, and other commonly tested areas
- Detailed career information, including college programs for specific jobs, requirements and qualifications, comprehensive job descriptions, and much more

Thousands of Satisfied Customers Can't be Wrong:

"It's like having the test in advance."
—Ms. J. Kennedy

"Better than the $200 6-week study courses being offered. After studying from dozens of books I would choose yours over any of the other companies."
—Mr. S. Frosh

"Best test-prep book I've used."
—Mr. H. Hernandez

Don't Delay!

To order any of these titles, fill in the quantities beside each book on the order form and mail your check/money order for the full amount* (please include $6.95 postage/handling for the first book and $1.00 for each additional book) to:

LearningExpress
Dept. A040
20 Academy Street
Norwalk, CT 06850

Or Call, **TOLL-FREE:**
1-888-551-JOBS, Dept. A040
to place a credit card order

LearningExpress books are also available in your local bookstore.

Please allow at least 2-4 weeks for delivery. Prices subject to change without notice.   *NY, MD, & CT residents add appropriate sales tax

Order Form

CALIFORNIA EXAMS
- ___ @ $35.00 CA Allied Health
- ___ @ $35.00 CA Corrections Officer
- ___ @ $35.00 CA Firefighter
- ___ @ $20.00 CA Law Enforcement Career Guide
- ___ @ $35.00 CA Police Officer
- ___ @ $30.00 CA Postal Worker
- ___ @ $35.00 CA State Police
- ___ @ $17.95 CBEST (California Basic Educational Skills Test)

NEW JERSEY EXAMS
- ___ @ $35.00 NJ Allied Health
- ___ @ $35.00 NJ Corrections Officer
- ___ @ $35.00 NJ Firefighter
- ___ @ $20.00 NJ Law Enforcement Career Guide
- ___ @ $35.00 NJ Police Officer
- ___ @ $30.00 NJ Postal Worker
- ___ @ $35.00 NJ State Police

TEXAS EXAMS
- ___ @ $17.95 TASP (Texas Academic Skills Program)
- ___ @ $32.50 TX Allied Health
- ___ @ $35.00 TX Corrections Officer
- ___ @ $35.00 TX Firefighter
- ___ @ $20.00 TX Law Enforcement Career Guide
- ___ @ $35.00 TX Police Officer
- ___ @ $30.00 TX Postal Worker
- ___ @ $29.95 TX Real Estate Exam
- ___ @ $30.00 TX State Police

NEW YORK EXAMS
- ___ @ $30.00 New York City Firefighter
- ___ @ $25.00 NYC Police Officer
- ___ @ $35.00 NY Allied Health
- ___ @ $35.00 NY Corrections Officer
- ___ @ $35.00 NY Firefighter
- ___ @ $20.00 NY Law Enforcement Career Guide
- ___ @ $30.00 NY Postal Worker
- ___ @ $35.00 NY State Police
- ___ @ $30.00 Suffolk County Police Officer

MASSACHUSETTS EXAMS
- ___ @ $30.00 MA Allied Health
- ___ @ $30.00 MA Police Officer
- ___ @ $30.00 MA State Police Exam

ILLINOIS EXAMS
- ___ @ $25.00 Chicago Police Officer
- ___ @ $25.00 Illinois Allied Health

FLORIDA EXAMS
- ___ @ $32.50 FL Allied Health
- ___ @ $35.00 FL Corrections Officer
- ___ @ $20.00 FL Law Enforcement Career Guide
- ___ @ $35.00 FL Police Officer
- ___ @ $30.00 FL Postal Worker

REGIONAL EXAMS
- ___ @ $29.95 AMP Real Estate Sales Exam
- ___ @ $29.95 ASI Real Estate Sales Exam
- ___ @ $30.00 Midwest Police Officer Exam
- ___ @ $30.00 Midwest Firefighter Exam
- ___ @ $17.95 PPST (Praxis I)
- ___ @ $29.95 PSI Real Estate Sales Exam
- ___ @ $25.00 The South Police Officer Exam
- ___ @ $25.00 The South Firefighter Exam

NATIONAL EDITIONS
- ___ @ $20.00 Allied Health Entrance Exams
- ___ @ $14.95 ASVAB (Armed Services Vocational Aptitude Battery): Complete Preparation Guide
- ___ @ $12.95 ASVAB Core Review
- ___ @ $17.95 Border Patrol Exam
- ___ @ $12.95 Bus Operator Exam
- ___ @ $15.00 Federal Clerical Exam
- ___ @ $12.95 Postal Worker Exam
- ___ @ $12.95 Sanitation Worker Exam
- ___ @ $17.95 Treasury Enforcement Agent Exam

NATIONAL CERTIFICATION & LICENSING EXAMS
- ___ @ $20.00 Cosmetology Licensing Exam
- ___ @ $20.00 EMT-Basic Certification Exam
- ___ @ $20.00 Home Health Aide Certification Exam
- ___ @ $20.00 Nursing Assistant Certification Exam
- ___ @ $20.00 Paramedic Licensing Exam

CAREER STARTERS
- ___ @ $14.95 Administrative Assistant/Secretary
- ___ @ $14.00 Civil Service
- ___ @ $14.95 Computer Technician
- ___ @ $14.95 Cosmetology
- ___ @ $14.95 EMT
- ___ @ $14.95 Firefighter
- ___ @ $14.95 Health Care
- ___ @ $14.95 Law Enforcement
- ___ @ $14.95 Paralegal
- ___ @ $14.95 Real Estate
- ___ @ $14.95 Retailing
- ___ @ $14.95 Teacher

To Order, Call TOLL-FREE: 1-888-551-JOBS, Dept. A040

Or, mail this order form with your check or money order* to:

LearningExpress, Dept. A040, 20 Academy Street, Norwalk, CT 06850

Please allow at least 2-4 weeks for delivery. Prices subject to change without notice   *NY, CT, & MD residents add appropriate sales tax

LearningExpress®
An Affiliate Company of Random House, Inc.